Articles

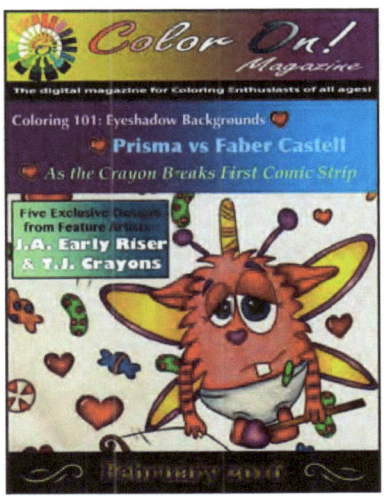

This month's cover:

Coloring design drawn by feature artists J.A. Early Riser & T.J. Crayons; colored by Renee Howell-Delgadillo.

Copyright © 2016 Tangitude Publications. All rights reserved. Illustrations in this volume are used with permission from the individual artists and illustrators. They hold all copyrights to their work. The designs in this book are intended for personal use only. No part of this publication may be reproduced or distributed in any form without written permission from Tangitude Publications and the illustrators (the copyright owners.)

Tangitude Publications

Editor-in-Chief
Mary J. Winters-Meyer

Marketing Marshal
Anisa A. Claire

Artists

J.A. Early Riser & T.J. Crayons
Alicia Nees
Karlon Douglas
Komfort Wiafe
Mary J. Winters-Meyer
Olivia Julius Dunggat
Penny Farthing Graphics
Rick St. Dennis
Sena Carroz
Valerie, Harry & the Fisch

Authors

Alex Whisman
Anisa A. Claire *(a.k.a J.A. Early Riser)*
Mary J. Winter-Meyer
Shelly Durham
Shelly Pfeiffer

Color On! Magazine is a digital magazine founded by Mary J. Winters-Meyer and Shyla Jannusch, published monthly by Tangitude Publications, P.O. Box 17623, Urbana, IL 61803-7623. For subscription information, visit our website at http://ColorOnMag.com.

All rights reserved except where expressly waived.

To make changes to your account online, go to ColorOnMag.com

ISBN: 0692659056
ISBN-13: 978-0692659052

From the Editor's Desk

WE'RE GOING TO have fun for February! Our feature artists, J.A. Early Riser and T.J. Crayons, have drawn us some amazing and fun exclusive designs for you to color, as well as sharing some samples from their Absur'd series of books. And we have the very first of our fun new comic strip, dreamed up for you by J.A and myself, featuring Marshal Early Riser and her sidekick Gallumphing Grammar Gal!

Of course, with February being a month for hearts, flowers and love, we have some Valentine's designs for you – both in a traditional flowery style, as well as fun, funky and unique styles from our contributing artists. We hope you enjoy coloring them as much as our coloring team! We also have designs for Mardi Gras, and a few other designs we hope you enjoy.

For our tutorial columns, Shelly Pfeiffer created a video showing how she uses eyeshadow to create some amazingly beautiful backgrounds. It's not as hard as it sounds! Then, Alex Whisman brings us an advanced tutorial showing us how to use Vaseline for blending colored pencils. And Anisa Claire compares Prismacolor Premier and Faber Castell pencils for us.

Color ON!

Mary J. Winters-Meyer

Editor-in-chief
Color On! Magazine

P.S. Check out the entries in our February cover contest online at ColorOnMag.com – it was incredibly difficult picking the final design for the cover. Everyone on our coloring team did an amazing job!

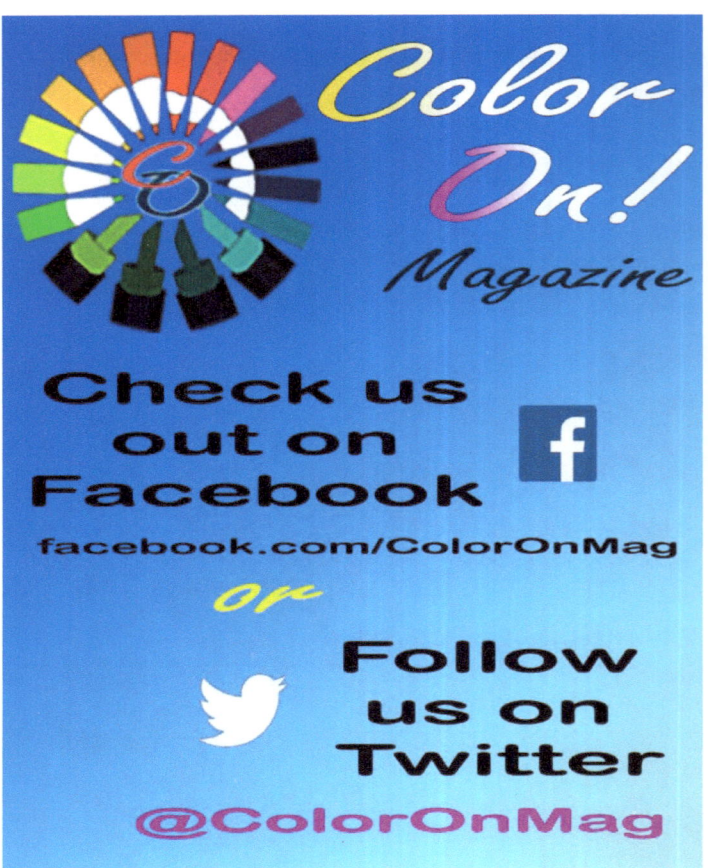

Color On! Magazine

Check us out on Facebook
facebook.com/ColorOnMag

or

Follow us on Twitter
@ColorOnMag

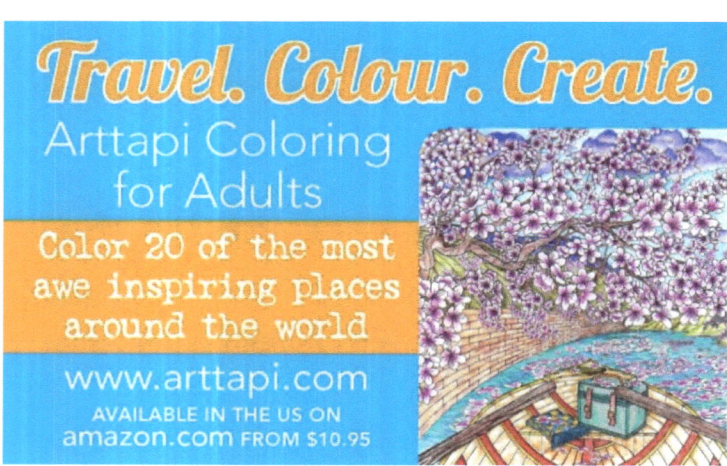

Travel. Colour. Create.
Arttapi Coloring for Adults
Color 20 of the most awe inspiring places around the world
www.arttapi.com
AVAILABLE IN THE US ON amazon.com FROM $10.95

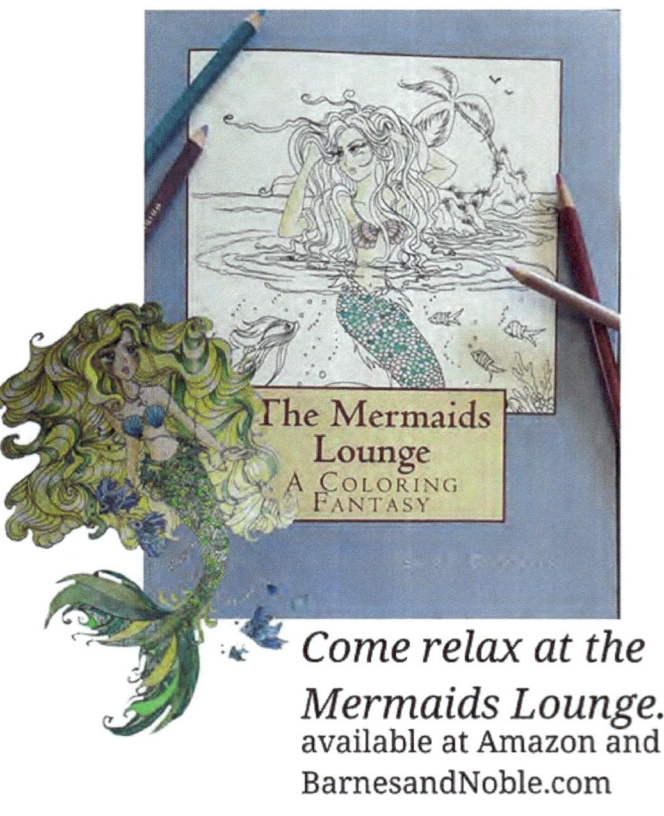

The Mermaids Lounge
A Coloring Fantasy

Come relax at the Mermaids Lounge.
available at Amazon and BarnesandNoble.com

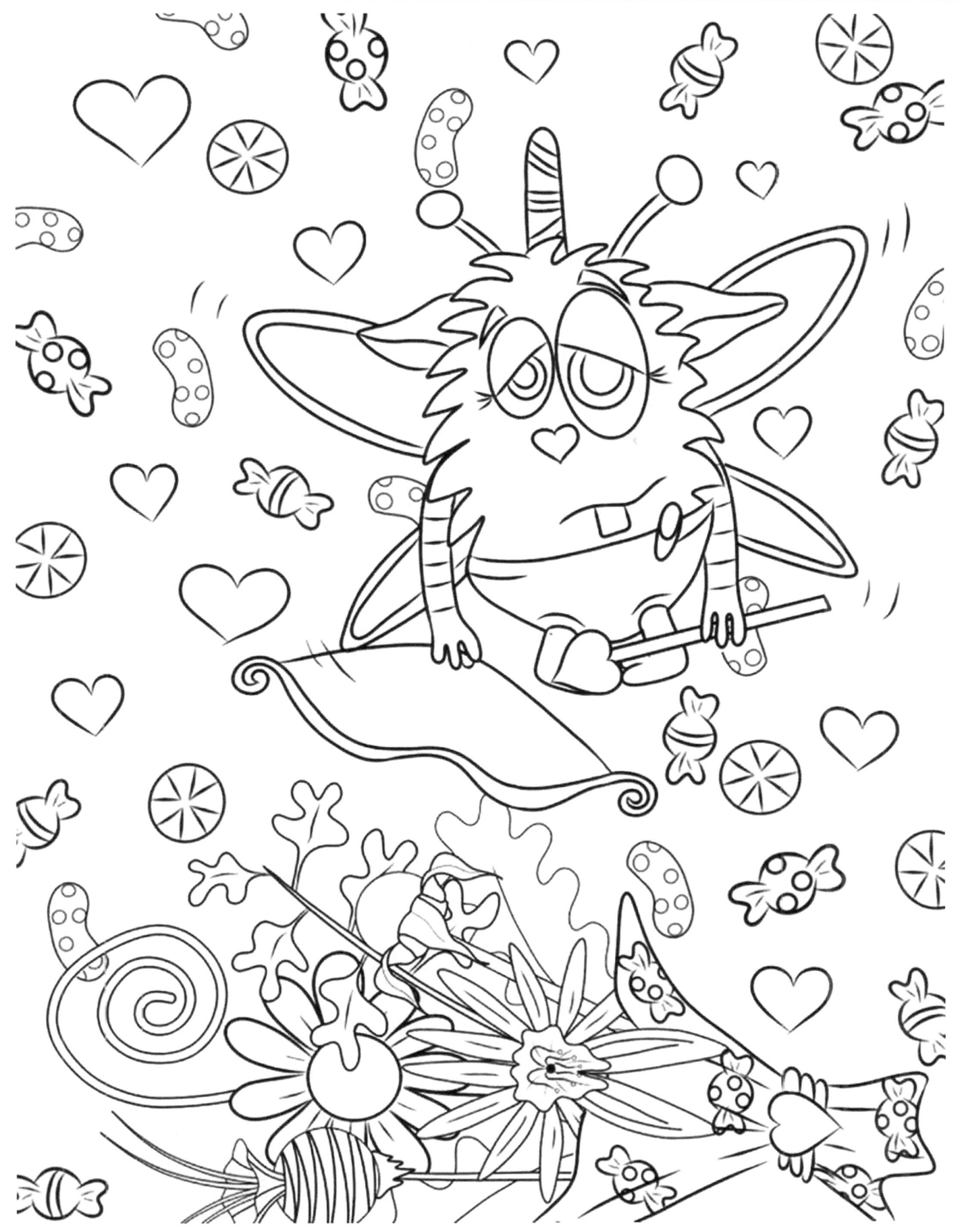

A chat with Absur'dians J.A. Early Riser and T.J. Crayons

By Mary J. Winters-Meyer

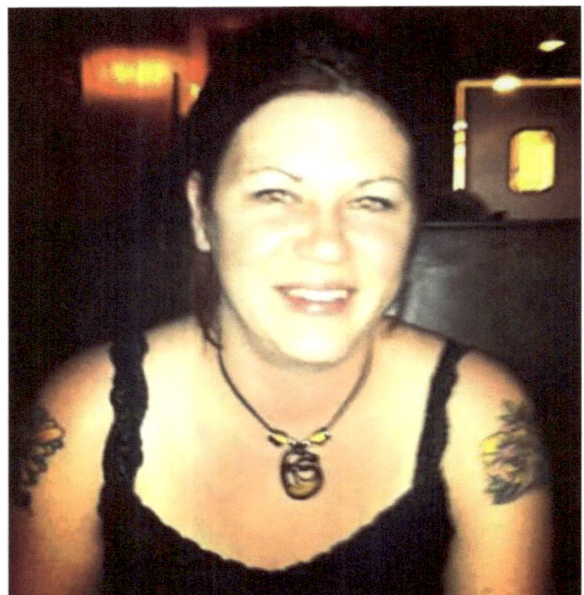

THIS MONTH WE explore the humorous worlds of Canadian writers and artists, Anisa (J.A. Early Riser) and Travis (T.J. Crayons.) J.A.'s unique brand of humor is brought to life in their Maniacal Confessions series of books, with feral faeries, sock monsters, warrior gnomes, drama llamas, sugar frenzies, Grumplestiltskins, and other characters that encourage colorists to use their craziest color combinations when coloring them. In this interview, they give us a peek into how they create their wacky coloring books!

Color On!: You have several writing-related online magazines. What made you add coloring books? Is there a connection?

J.A. EARLY RISER: There is a connection, actually. I'd been writing journal entries as J.A. Early Riser for a few years and always wanted to do something with them, but could never figure out exactly what. Travis (T.J. Crayons) and I discussed making a zombie survival guide, or an illustrated comic-type book, but the ideas never seemed quite right. Then, one day, my friend Juanita, who is mainly responsible for talking us into doing coloring books, came to town and asked if we could check Chapters for adult coloring books. I told her, good luck... that I'd been searching for such a beast my entire life and had never found any. Of course, I had no idea it was trending at the time.

I joined a few coloring groups, actually the very first one I joined was Adult Coloring Group. I was totally inspired by everything I saw and then it hit me... why not do an activity coloring book and use my J.A. Early Riser alter ego. So that's what we did. The first book, Maniacal Confessions, was released at the end of July, 2015.

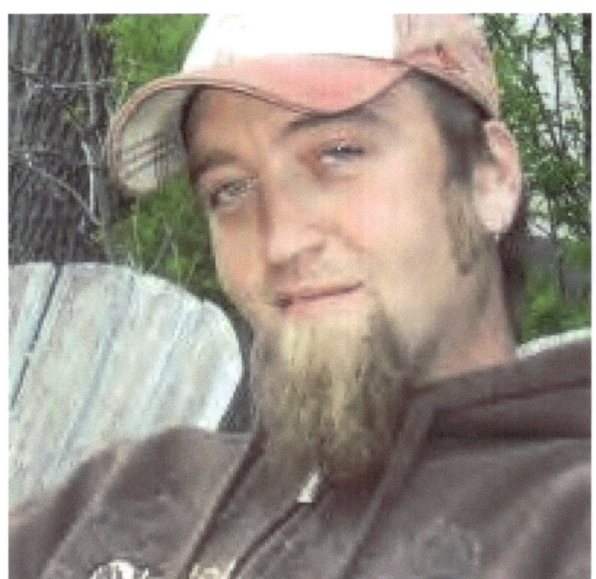

T.J. CRAYONS: My response to Anisa when she first approached me about doing coloring books together was... "Seriously?? Coloring books?? For adults?! Hahaha!" At the time, I didn't really know that was a thing. But then I thought back to how many times when I wanted to color, I had to buy books with pictures of big trains with happy faces on them and giant bounding cartoon dinosaurs. That sort of killed my drive for coloring. So the thought of making something that I would want to color was very appealing. We were lucky enough to get in when the adult coloring craze was still sort of in its infancy. I'm glad we did because it has grown into quite a massive following now.

Color On!: Most of your books have 2 versions – a JUST coloring book, and a combined coloring and activity book. Tell us about them. Why did you choose to release them like that?

J.A. EARLY RISER: We did a lot of market research before we released. There were a few things we noticed... First of all, there were a lot of complaints about the cover picture not being in the book, so we made sure to include our cover. The next thing we noticed was a decent sized demand for single sided pages. People who use pencil crayons don't mind the double sided books, but people who color mainly with markers can't use the double sided books. That's when we decided to release a Just Coloring version on top of the Activity version. The activity version really explains all of the characters and their stories and there are different activities plus bonus coloring sheets in it.

Another reason we released the Just Coloring version is because of the price difference. We wanted to offer a more affordable version of the book. Because the activity books have pages printed in color, and it's much longer than the Just Coloring version, Amazon forces us to list them at a minimum of $16.85 USD.

Color On!: What can you tell us about your experiences being a coloring book artist and the skills required to build a successful following online?

J.A. EARLY RISER: Hmmm. Not sure about the skills part, to be honest. We just sort of... jumped in and went with it. We spend a lot of time interacting with people in the coloring groups and take the time to comment on their pictures, especially if it's one of our pictures that they've posted. We both enjoy just being in the communities and hanging out with everyone who colors. It's a lot of fun.

The experience has been incredible. Drawing is actually a secondary thing for me. I mainly write, which is another reason I wanted to do the activity books – so I could combine both. Travis mainly draws, but he also writes poetry, so we're a great team for this kind of thing. We're both really enjoying ourselves so far.

Color On!: How do you create your art? Do you create digitally or with pen and pencil? Tell us about your process for creating new work.

T.J. CRAYONS: I draw digitally, using an art app on my iPad. I spent a lot of time drawing as a teenager and then stopped for a long time. Recently, I picked it up when Anisa decided to open Writer's Carnival. She asked me to do all the art on the site and I thought, sure, why not... Haha. I've learned a lot since then.

Anisa typically draws with pencil and paper and then traces it digitally so that our pictures are in the same format. We didn't do that for the first book but have for the rest of them.

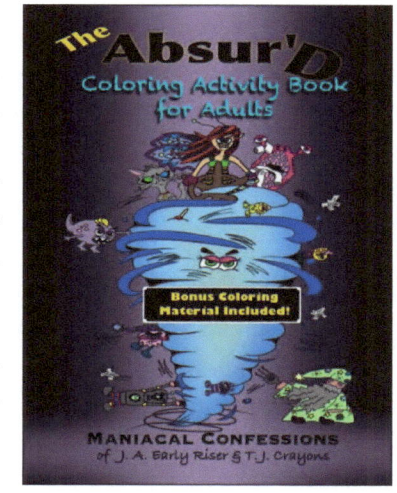

I struggled a little bit at first with the humor aspect of it. I've never been great with cartoon characters or coming up with crazy ideas. My focus was more on the patterns, covers and structures. Anisa would mainly brainstorm the nutty characters and scenarios. Eventually, though, I became a part of that process more and have been dipping into drawing my own Absur'D characters, as well.

Color On!: When coloring your own art, what is your favorite medium(s)?

T.J. CRAYONS: I definitely prefer pencil crayons. I've tried markers and gel pens, they're fun, but I can't shade very well with them.

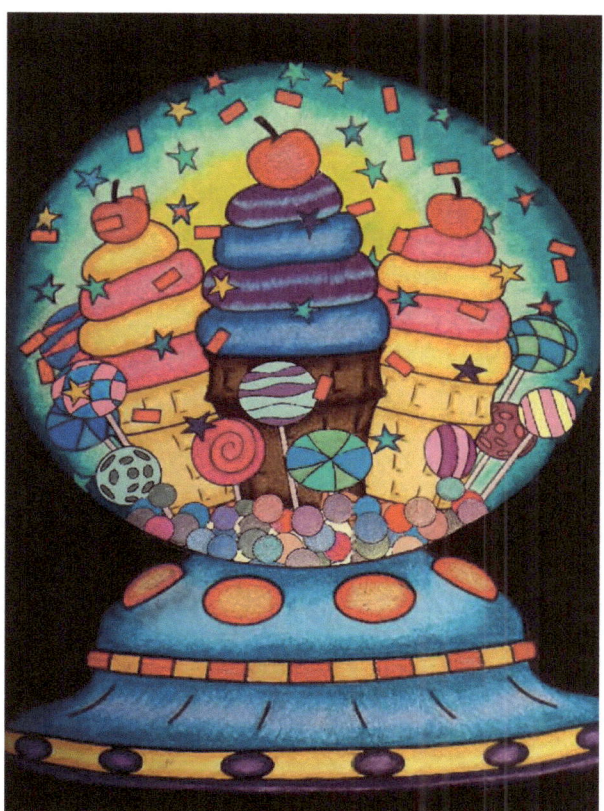

J.A. EARLY RISER: I love EVERYTHING! Hah! Pencil crayons, gel pens, markers, pastels .. anything I can get my hands on, I use... even highlighters!

Color On!: Do you enjoy relaxing with coloring books by other artists? If so, do you have a favorite artist or book?

J.A. EARLY RISER: Oh yeah, definitely. Hmmm... I have a few favorites! Well, yours, for starters, Mary! [Editor's note: *Dragons, Knots, Bots and More!*] I also love Coloring on the Edge (Karlon Douglas), Narwhalidays (Tracey Johnston), Chroma Tomes (especially their Gnome ones), Color with Komfort: Mind's Eye of a Gypsy, and then some of the bigger ones would be Doodle Invasion, Unicorns are Jerks, the Game of Thrones book. I'm a huge fan of Rick St. Dennis – I absolutely love his work – and From the Broken Mind of Joe's Ink. I could go on and on, but that's a few of them. Oh, and I really like a lot of the artists that have been published in Color On! Magazine, to be 100% honest. I really enjoyed the November issue with Ellen Million.

Color On!: What color or colors do you most love to work with?

T.J. CRAYONS: Greens and blues and yellows to reds.

J.A. EARLY RISER: I'm really not a fan of red... I know, I know. But it's true. I rarely use it. I love purples and turquoises. Most recently, I've been enjoying oranges and yellows.

Color On!: Tell us a little bit about your art. Do you have a favorite piece that you created? Do you create other art besides designs for coloring books?

T.J. CRAYONS: Oh. Tough question. My favorite so far is probably the Frenzy Fabricator in our newest book, Candy Coated Kaos. I love the little character's that are hidden in Anisa's head that she brings to life on her pages. They seem to come in extra handy for our latest book, Candy Coated Kaos. I was a big fan of the Feral Fairy Hoarder in Maniacal Confessions and Angry Chicken Mob in the same book. I do the covers for Reader's Carnival and Long Story Short magazines and all the site art on Writer's Carnival, Long Story Short and Maniacal Confessions. I also design book covers for people.

J.A. EARLY RISER: Not sure I can pick a favorite! I know my favorites so far from Travis are Grumpy Flowers in Maniacal Confessions, the Octopus Ride in Carnival Carnage, the Ice Cream Globe in Candy Kaos and Grumplestiltskin in Feral Fairy Tales. For my own picture... I think it's Granny and the Big Sad Wolf in Feral Fairy Tales. Other than Absur'D, no, I don't really do much else for art. I'm more of a writer. Well, unless planning parties for people and hand making all the decorations counts. Haha.

Color On!: Other than creating coloring book art, what interesting hobbies or activities do you enjoy?

J.A. EARLY RISER: Reading, reading and more reading. Did I mention reading? Haha. Writing stories, playing guitar, playing video games, camping, coloring, weird arts and crafts, animals (is that a hobby? Because I have a lot of them!), gardening, baking sometimes.

T.J. CRAYONS: Woodworking, writing poetry, camping, playing guitar, coloring, building the perfect campfire, playing video games, drawing.

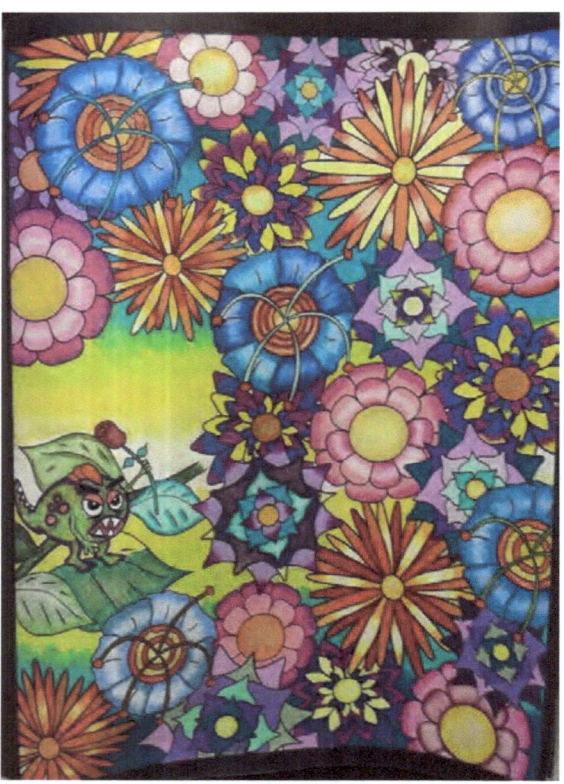

Color On!: Have you had any memorable responses to your art work from collectors?

T.J. CRAYONS: Yes. We've had some great responses from the pictures we do from the coloring books. Honestly didn't imagine this would go any further than a little hobby project, but so far the response has been pretty amazing.

J.A. EARLY RISER: Too many to list! It's been a surreal experience. I was really nervous when we put the first book out, thinking nobody would be interested, but I couldn't be happier with the response so far. It's been incredible.

Color On!: If you had to choose one superpower, what would it be?

T.J. CRAYONS: Oh, that's easy. Flying. No question. Ever since I was a kid, that's all I've wanted to do.

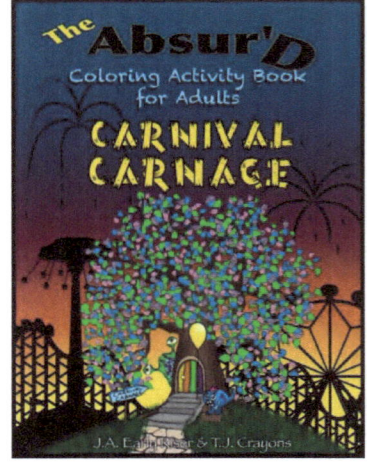

J.A. EARLY RISER: I'd definitely want to be able to time travel or something. That would be pretty awesome.

Color On!: Who is your favorite artist or artists?

T.J. CRAYONS: That's an impossible answer. I really like Karlon Douglas and Rick St. Dennis.

J.A. EARLY RISER: I already answered above, but if we're talking just art in general... Brian Froud, for sure.

Color On!: Is there some person, place or thing that inspires you when you are creating your art?

T.J. CRAYONS: Probably not really any one thing. As far as influences go, though, I'm a big fan of Dr. Seuss and always have been. I love the wacky pictures, but more importantly love the way he writes.

J.A. EARLY RISER: Hmmm. Not really. I live, eat and breathe humor. Love it. Anything that makes me laugh, or others laugh, that's my go to. So I'm constantly thinking about the weirdest things I can possibly think of and that's where I draw my inspiration from.

Color On!: Tell us about your plans for 2016. Are there other books being planned?

T.J. CRAYONS: Oh, most definitely. I think each book gets a little better than the last and Anisa and I have some more ideas in our head that we'd love to put to paper.

J.A. EARLY RISER: Way to not spill the beans, hey, Travis? Haha! We're thinking about doing another book in the Faerie Trimmings line, possibly Wizard Wares. Then we'd like to do Baby Absur'Dians and a holiday edition of Absur'D featuring Christmas, Easter, Valentine's Day, New Years and Halloween.

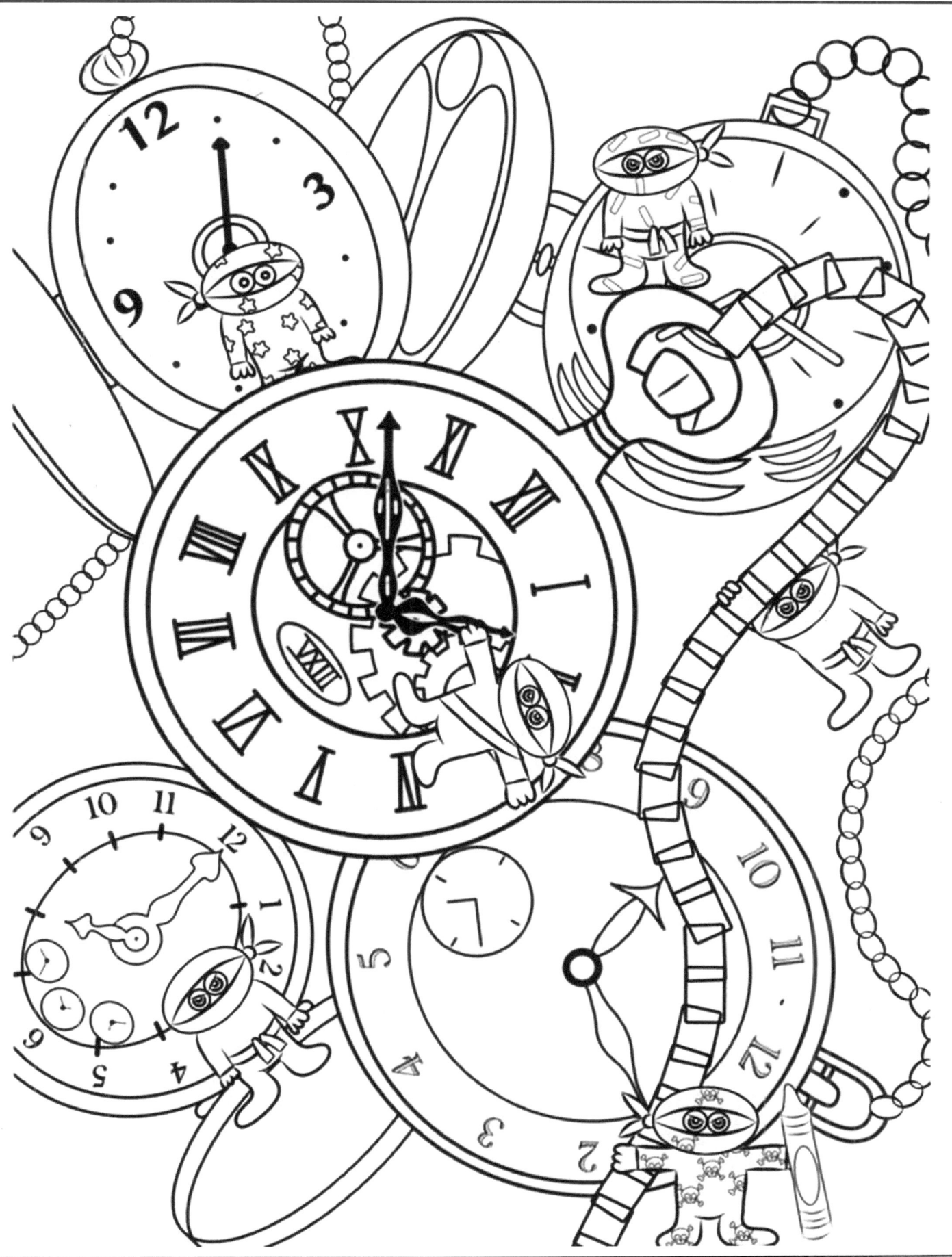

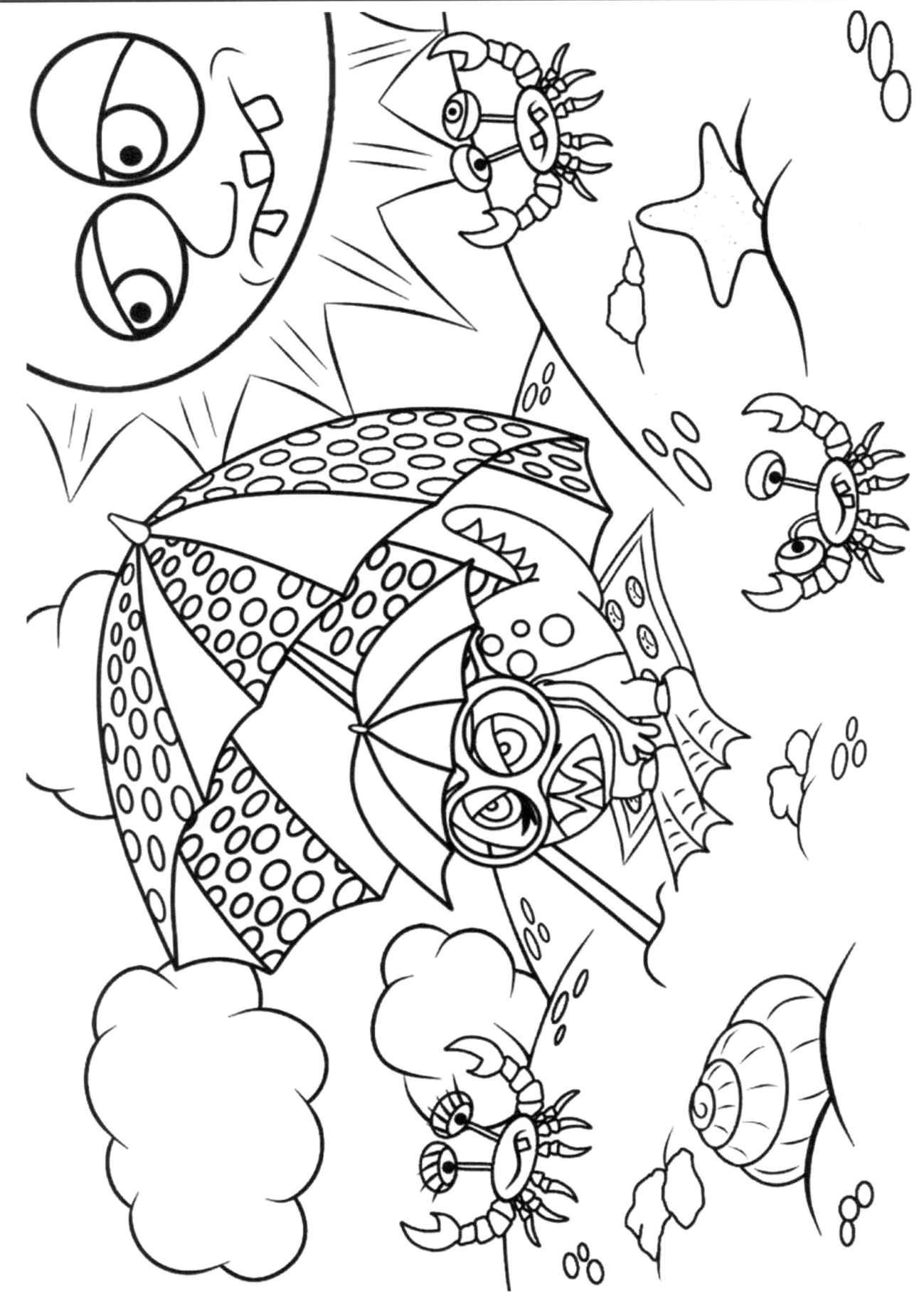

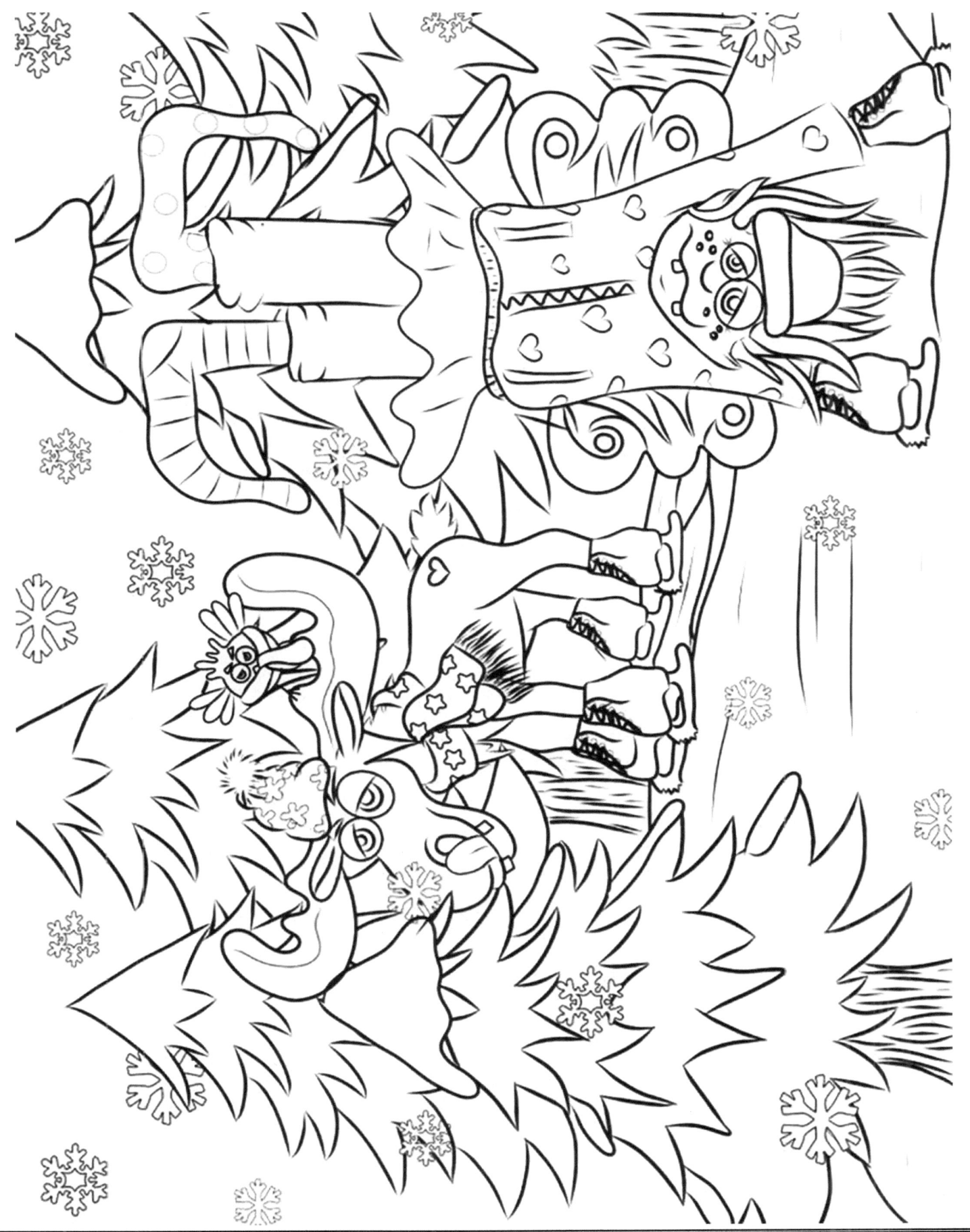

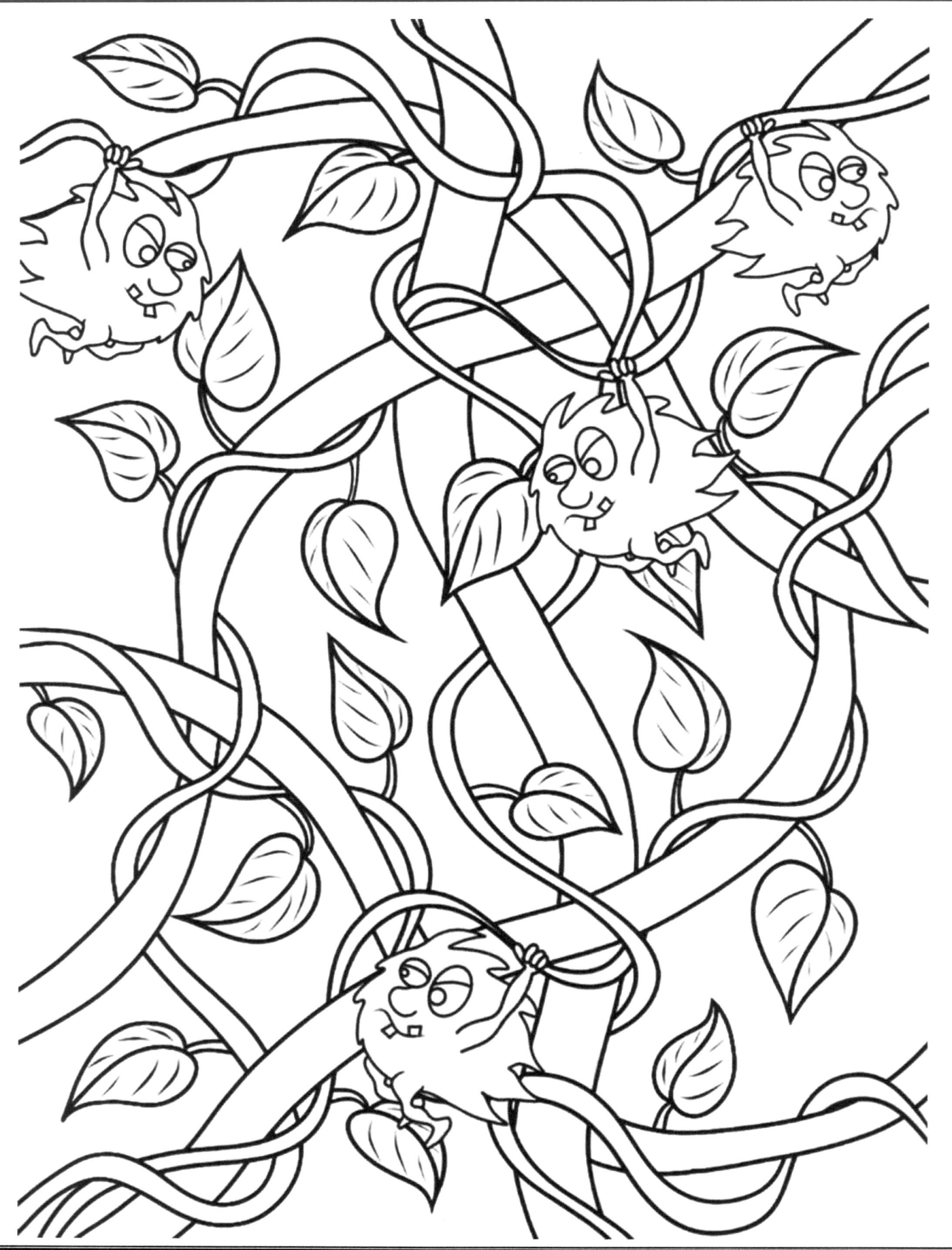

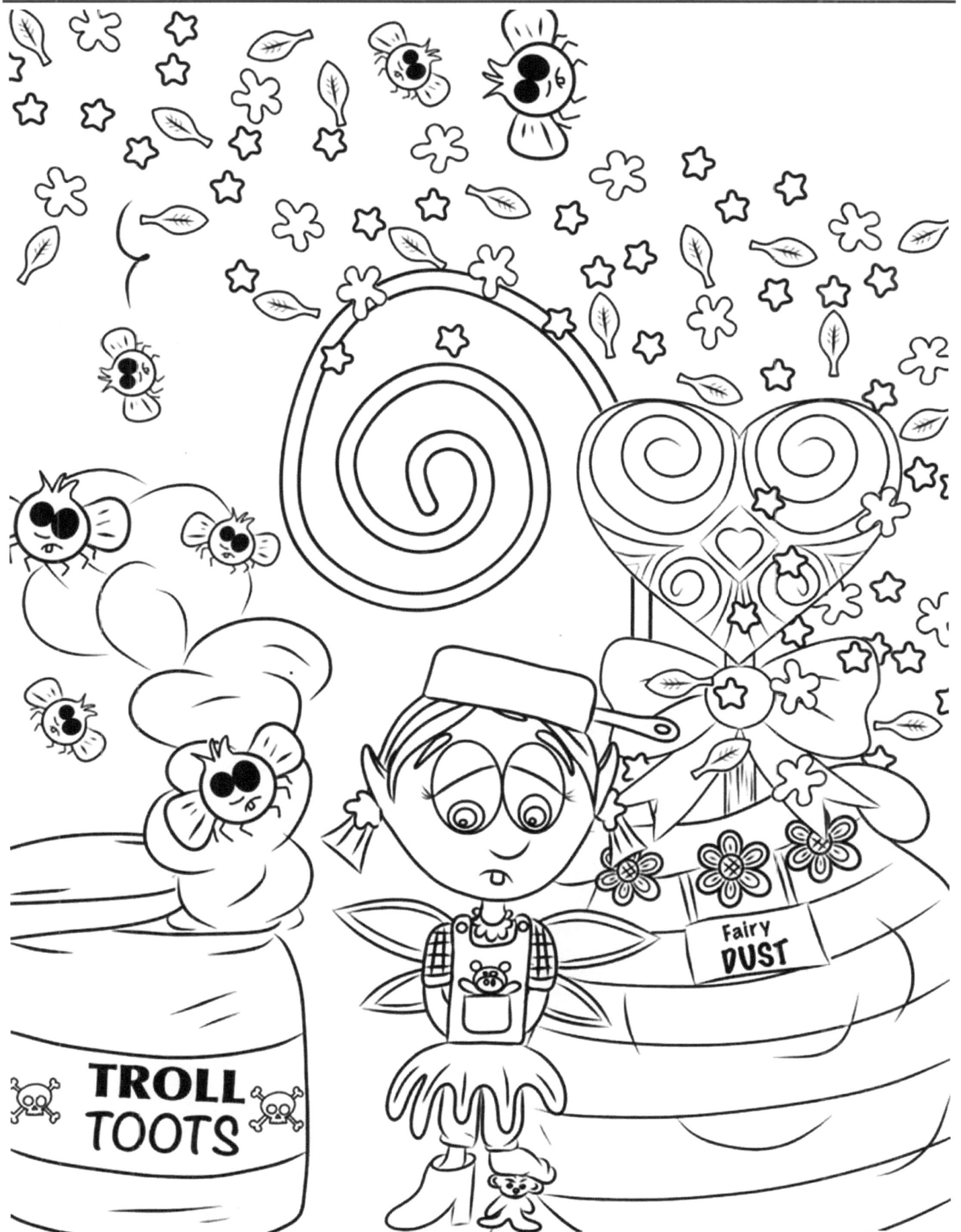

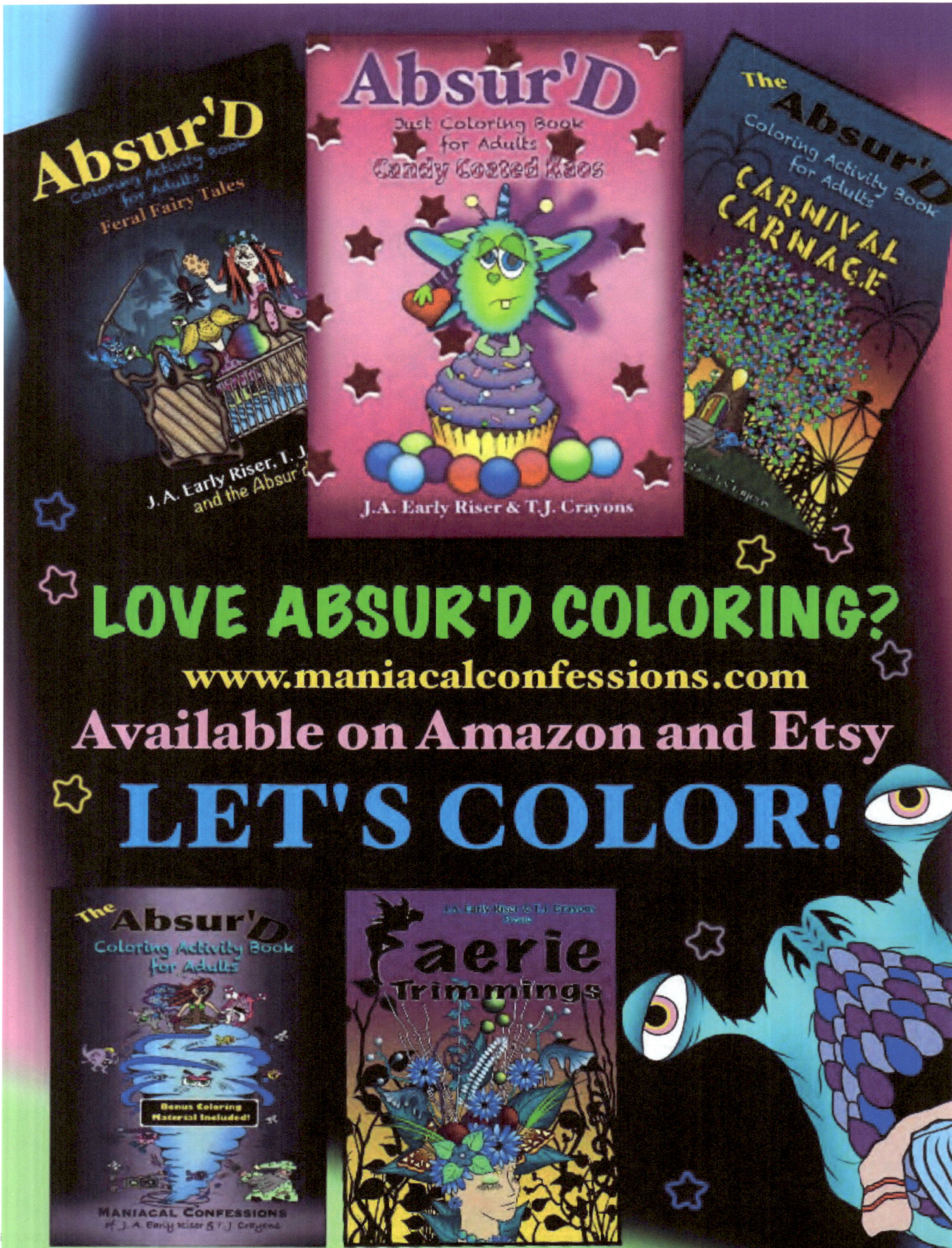

Coloring 101: Eyeshadow Backgrounds

Shelly Pfeiffer and Mary J. Winters-Meyer

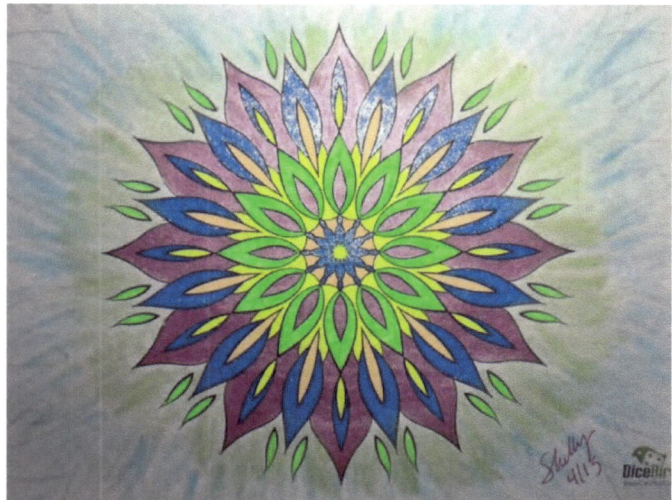

SHELLY PFEIFFER RECORDED a video for us this month showing how she and her mom use eyeshadow to create lovely backgrounds on the designs she colors. Watch the video online (http://tinyurl.com/Coloring101Eyeshadow) or read the instructions here to learn how she does it!

Why eyeshadow, you ask? Well, I'm sure most of us ladies have eyeshadow languishing in our makeup drawers. Colors we don't like, or that are old enough we don't want to use them on our delicate eyelids. A clever colorist or two decided to try using them on a coloring design, and shared her results. It gives you a delicate look reminiscent of pastels. If you don't happen to have eyeshadow sitting around, you don't have to purchase an expensive set from a major beauty brand. Check out your local dollar store!

Materials

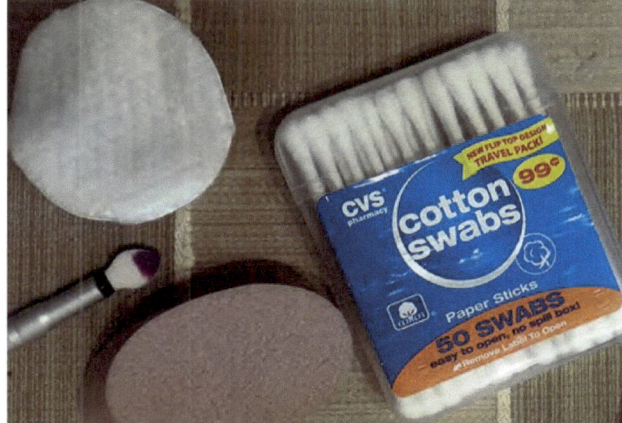

In addition to the actual eyeshadow, you'll need something to lay down the color. The easiest, of course, is to just use the eyeshadow brush that comes with the eyeshadow. If you've lost that tiny little sponge-tip brush – or

the sponge tip has been destroyed over time - your dollar store probably has some of those as well. Or, if you want something easier to hold, pick up some makeup sponges, or use cotton pads, cotton balls or q-tips. You could even use paper towels or your finger in a pinch!

Techniques

There are two basic techniques you can use to lay down the color. Both are simple, but can give you some great effects.

Dabbing

Dabbing involves tapping the color onto the paper with a light touch. In this sample image, I've dabbed using a light purple shade. Don't worry if your first few dabs seem to lay down too light of a color. Just continue to dab more color onto the paper until you get a depth of color you like. I put down four-five layers in this sample to get a purple I liked. You may also notice that some eyeshadows put down a deeper color with fewer layers than others. The black color in later examples only required a couple layers to give the result in the images.

Dabbing works best using a tool with a distinct tip, so that you lay down small dots of color with each "dab." You don't have to limit yourself to a single color. In this next example, I used a black and a gold color. The image doesn't show it very well, but the gold actually has a shimmer to it, like many eyeshadows.

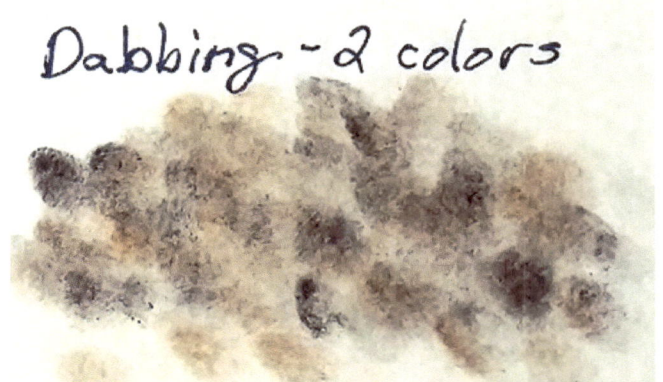

That's one of the great things about using eyeshadow instead of pastels. Pastels can be used in a similar fashion, but don't generally have the same range of shimmery or sparkly colors.

Brushing

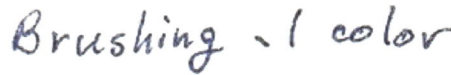

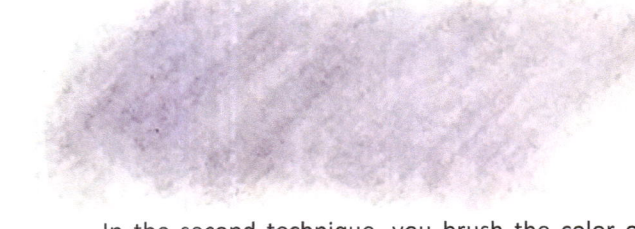

In the second technique, you brush the color onto the paper using light strokes. Depending on the tool you use, you can lay down narrow strokes or brush over large areas. You can also leave the strokes as individual streaks of color as in the example Shelly created for her video, or you can smooth the strokes together for a more solid coverage as I did here.

As with the dabbing, you can use just a single color, or combine colors for other effects. As with the dabbing, I used both black and gold on this example.

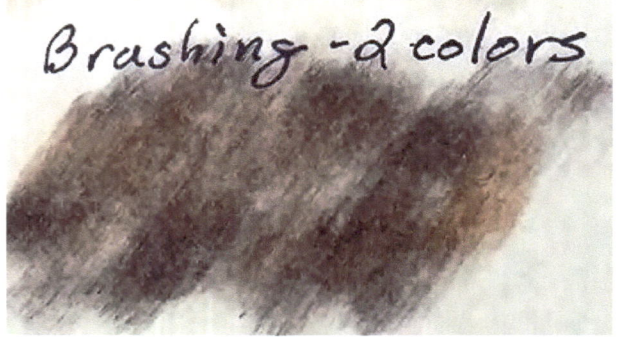

You can also experiment with combining dabbing and brushing. For my final sample, I brushed down a solid layer of purple, then dabbed both black and gold over it. You can see how the purple underneath changes the look of both the black and the gold.

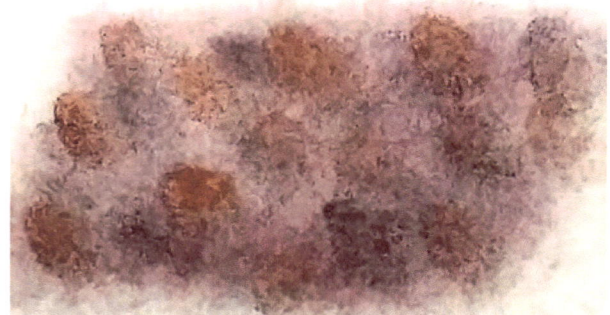

See, simple! So dig into your makeup drawer or bag, pull out those old or unused colors, and have fun with it!

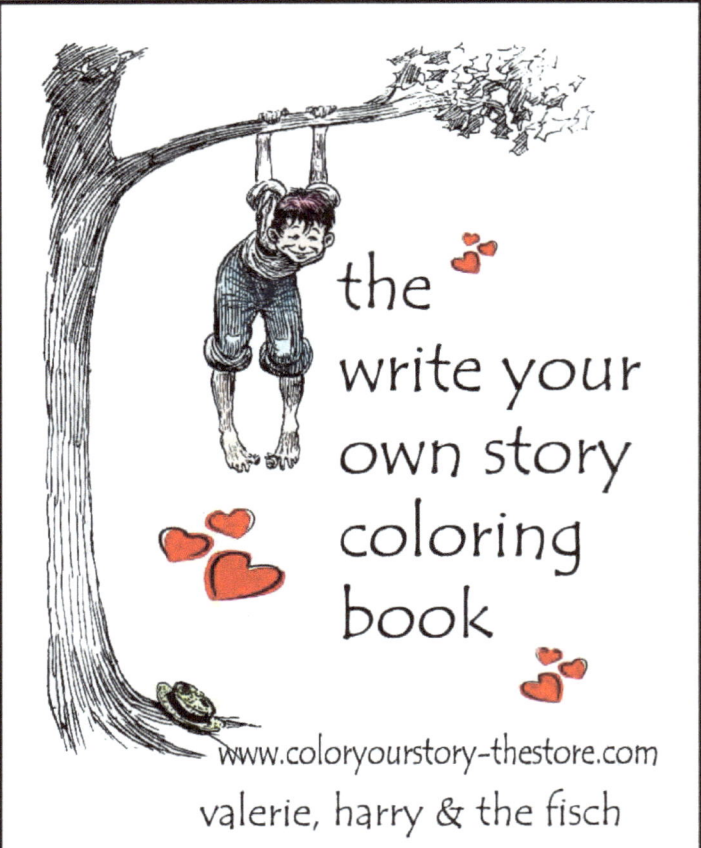

the write your own story coloring book

www.coloryourstory-thestore.com
valerie, harry & the fisch

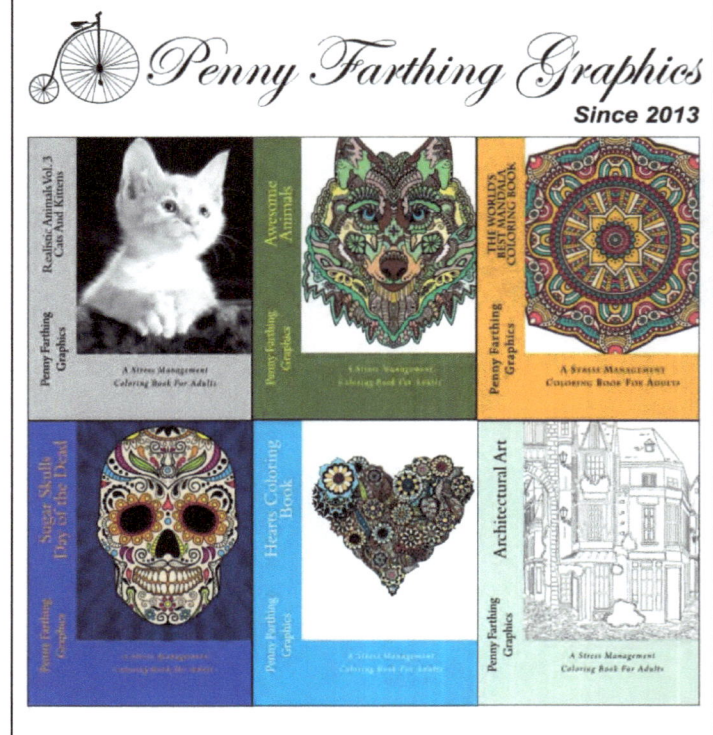

https://www.facebook.com/pennyfarthingcoloringbooks
http://www.amazon.com/author/pennyfarthinggraphics

Coloring for Seniors

An interview with Shelly Durham

Anisa A. Claire

"WE DIDN'T GET any funding for art supplies this year. There just wasn't anything available in our limited budget." Those were the words spoken by the director of American Senior Living, a nursing home in Clarksville, Indiana, close to where Shelly Durham resides. It was then Shelly decided to take matters into her own hands, providing nearly 300 coloring books and almost 250 boxes of colored pencils.

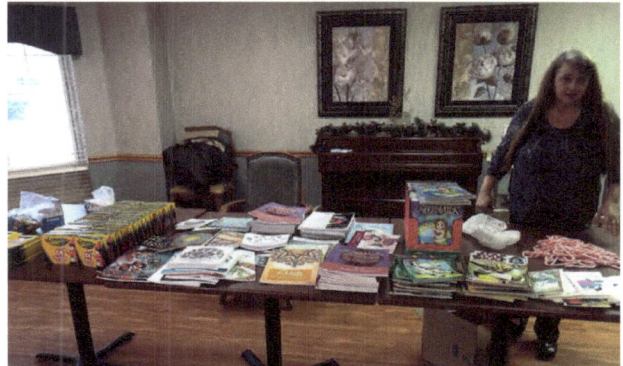

Color On!: What made you approach the director in the first place?

SHELLY DURHAM: My boyfriend, Dwayne, works at the facility as an aide, specializing in Alzheimer's and hospice care. He would often come home, talking about how lonely the residents were. He told me a story one night about an Alzheimer's patient and how he'd given her a coloring book. He told me it immediately calmed her down, when nothing else could. The next day, I gave him some more books to bring into work with him. After that, I decided to make it a mission to try and bring them a little joy.

Color On!: After deciding you were going to help these seniors, what steps did you take?

SHELLY DURHAM: I admin for a few different coloring groups on Facebook. The size of the groups ranges from 1000 to 35,000 members. On average, I receive 60 to 80 coloring books per month to review from coloring book artists. What we don't use for giveaways in the groups, I donate to the seniors.

On top of the reviewing copies, I decided to start a GoFund Me account and hit up the members to see if they'd be interested in donating a few dollars to help out.

Color On!: How much were you able to raise?

SHELLY DURHAM: We were able to raise over 600 dollars through donations from Facebook coloring group members in just under two months. The money was then used to purchase crayons, colored pencils, erasers, pencil sharpeners, and candy canes. We also received over 150 Christmas cards that members colored. The coloring books came from books I reviewed and donations sent from coloring book artists and colorists. We were also able to pick up some children's coloring books for the Alzheimer's patients. It was truly incredible to see how much can be accomplished when people come together with a singular purpose in mind.

Color On!: All of your hard work is finally coming to end and you get to go and deliver all of those supplies you collected. Describe the experience.

SHELLY DURHAM: As the gift bags were passed out, you could just see the joy that the coloring supplies brought. One woman exclaimed, "Praise Jesus, you have no idea how much this means to me." It makes your heart feel good to make so many people happy, and I can't believe how many hugs I got that day. They were remembered and blessed by strangers...all of you that made this possible. As we walked out of the nursing home, passing the open doors of the residents, just about every one of them was sitting up and coloring. It brought tears to my eyes.

Coloring is relaxing, helps to alleviate pain, depression and so many other medical problems, plus it makes us happy. I couldn't imagine what it would be like to sit endlessly, for hours, when all I had to look forward to was my next meal, for someone to tell me when to wake up, go to bed, when to shower or when I could walk outside. Coloring will give the seniors a choice and a wonderful distraction. This is the first time that they have had books and crayons in their room and they can color whenever they want. Before, coloring was a planned activity, where they met in a group. They all shared the colored pencils, markers and crayons. Now they have the opportunity to color whenever they want. I gave the director my phone number, so she could call when someone needs a new book. I don't always have donations to get the colored pencils, but I always have books and if push came to shove, I could print off some of our free coloring pages.

Color On!: That's really incredible, Shelly! What a beautiful accomplishment. Are you working on another project or is there a way people can donate to keep supplies coming into the home?

SHELLY DURHAM: Our next campaign is to provide coloring supplies to Veteran's at the VA Hospital in Louisville and if we get enough donations, we will include the Veterans in Fort Knox, Kentucky. The GoFundMe account was just started: https://www.gofundme.com/gjhfze2s. It's a great cause and we hope it is as successful as our Christmas campaign.

Color On!: We're wishing you the best! Thank you for starting this project and making the world a little better for the seniors at American Senior Living.

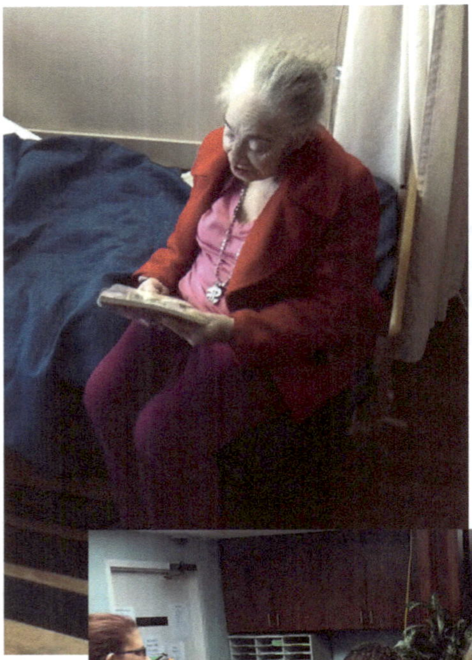

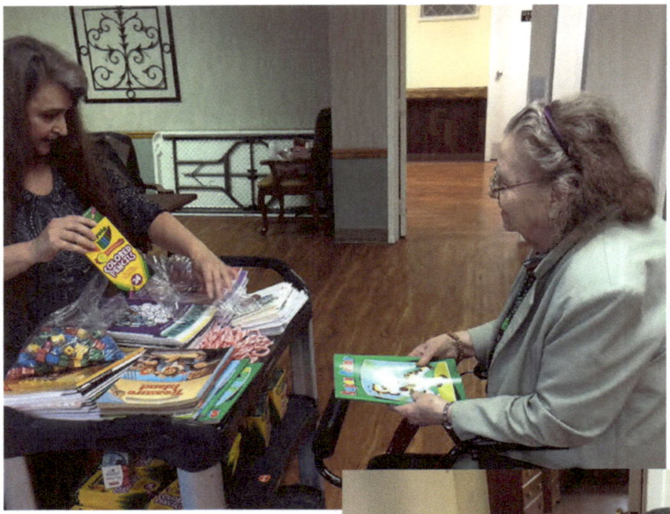

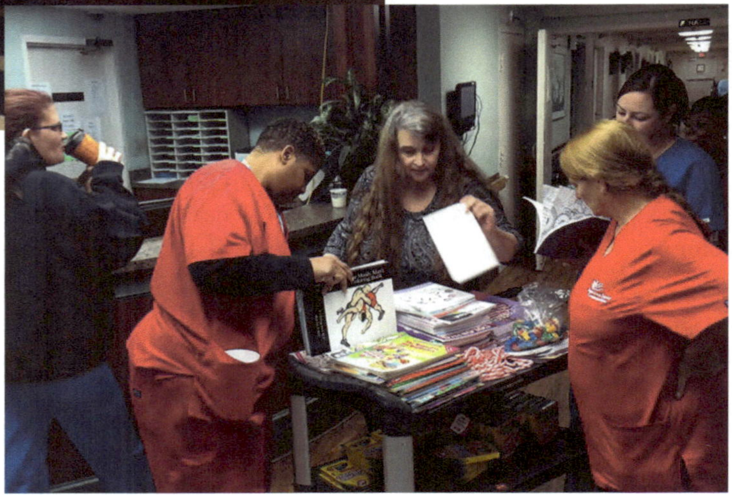

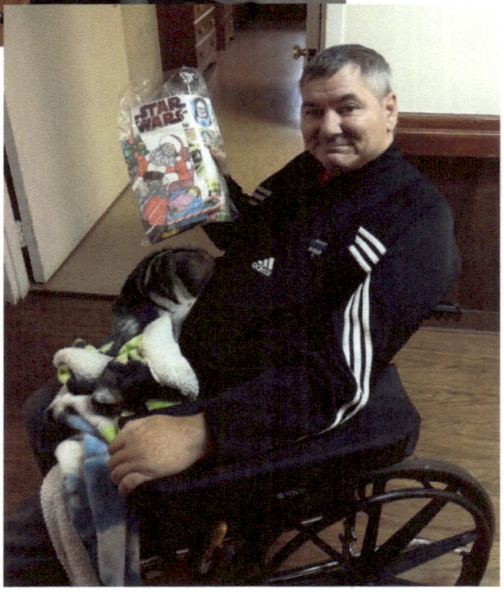

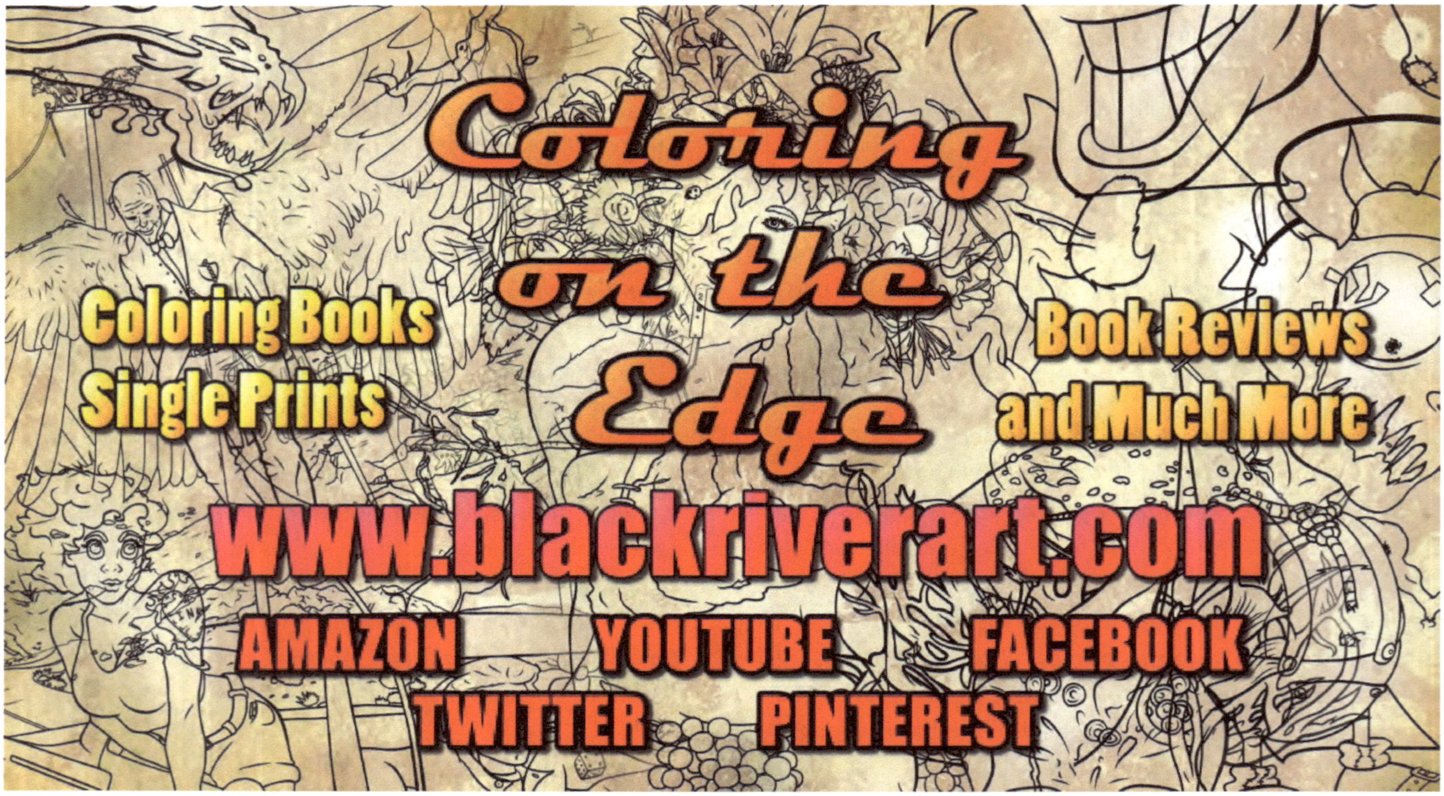

Coloring on the Edge

Coloring Books
Single Prints

Book Reviews
and Much More

www.blackriverart.com

AMAZON   YOUTUBE   FACEBOOK
TWITTER   PINTEREST

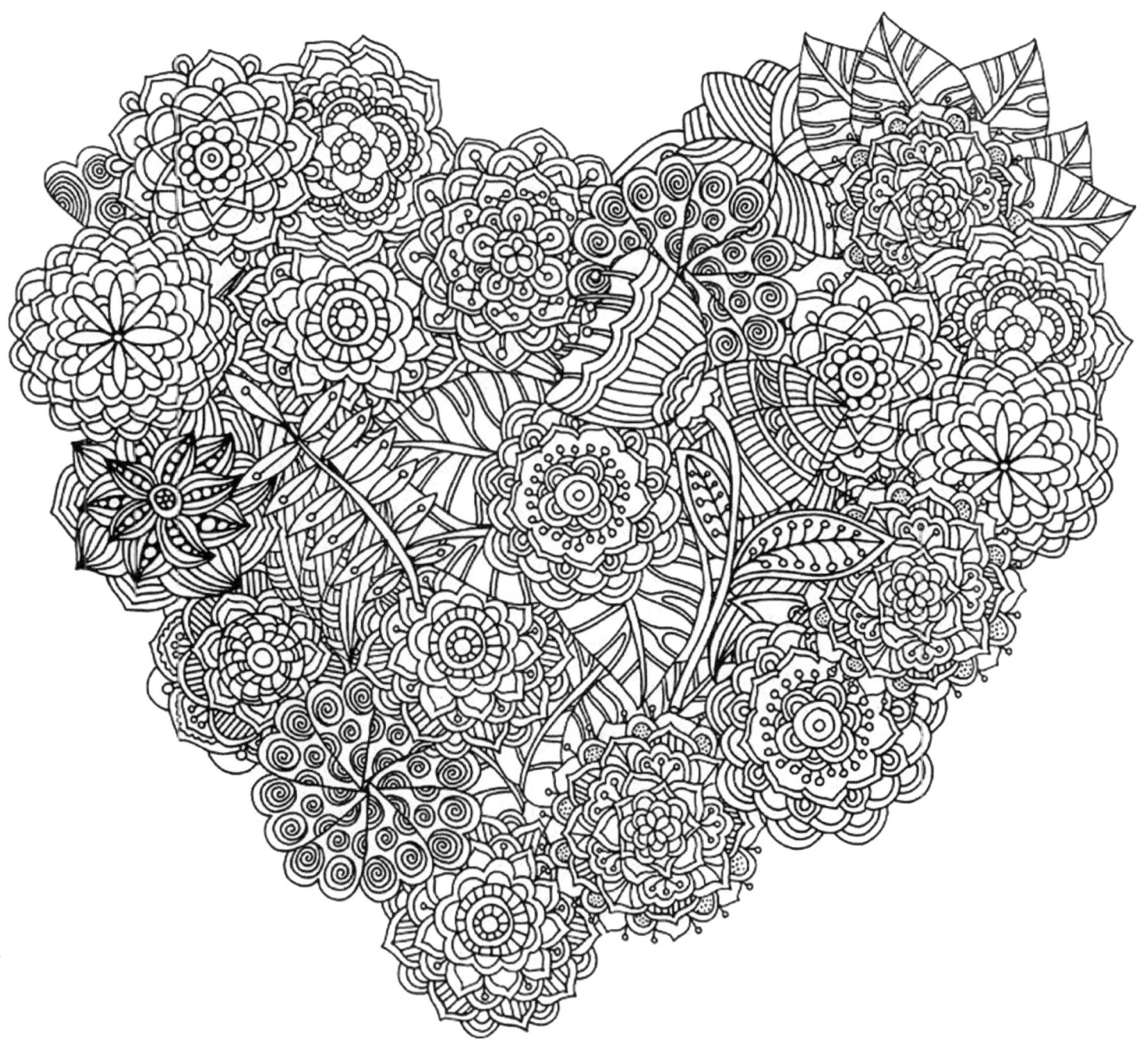

**HEARTS COLORING BOOK
PENNY FARTHING GRAPHICS**

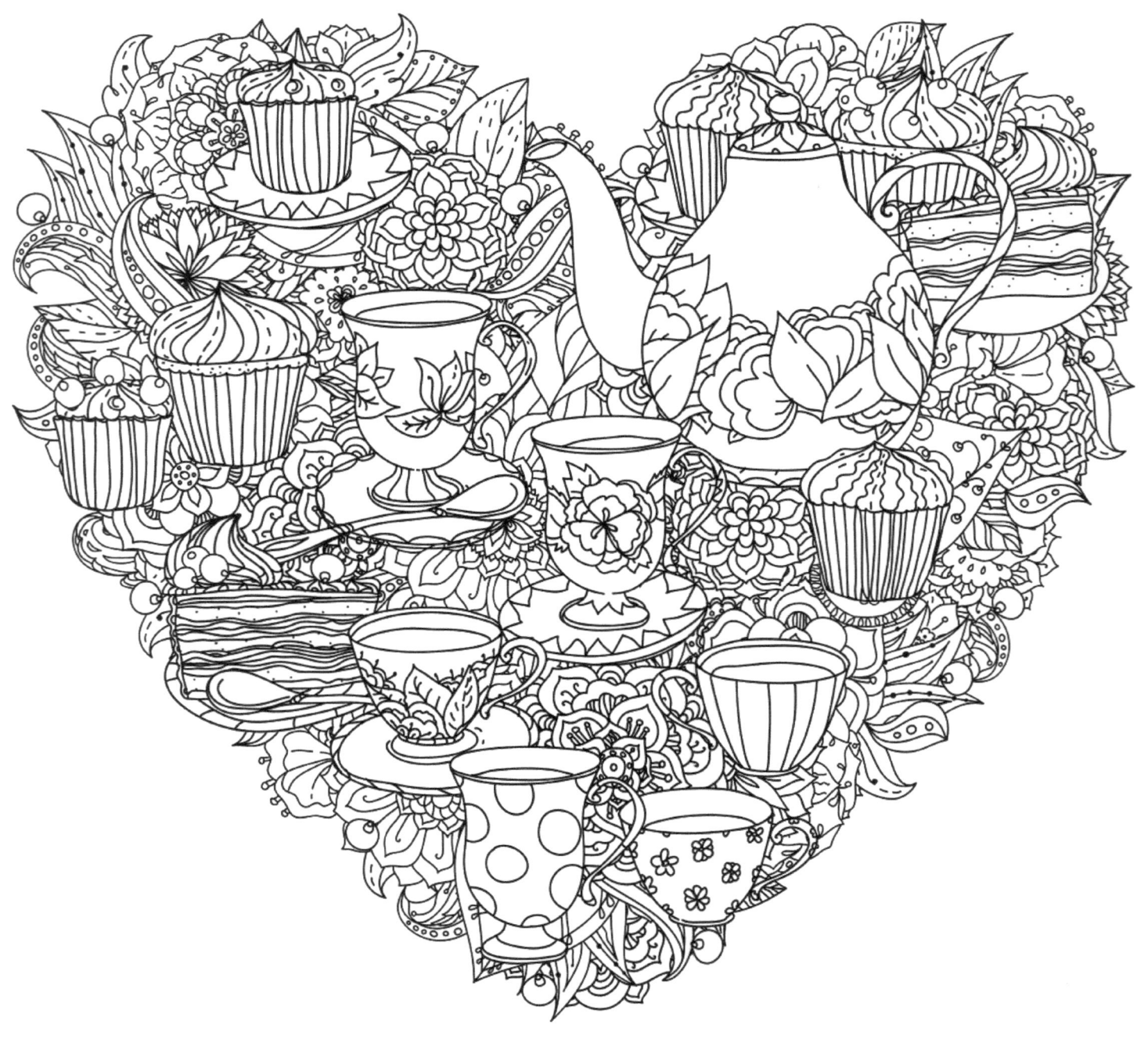

HEARTS COLORING BOOK
PENNY FARTHING GRAPHICS

Coloring 201: You Do WHAT with Vaseline?!?

by Alex Whisman

WHAT YOU USE to color and to make your pictures look their best will partly depend on the media you use, your budget, personal style, time constraints and if you have any health or pain issues. It also depends on what your final vision for your picture is. There are a lot of unusual coloring tips out on the wonderfully world wide web. You could easily browse YouTube for hours learning all of them.

I mainly color with pencils. I like the look they give a picture. I like being able to create new colors by blending them. I like being able to put them on lightly or darker and I like their feel as they go onto the paper. I use Faber Castell entry level Aquarelle water color pencils and their higher quality Albrecht Durer water color pencils. They give me a nice wide range of options for color.

However, unless you buy really expensive pencils or put down a few layers of color, sometimes colored pencils don't quite have the depth of color that a felt tip or a gel pen does. As we saw in the January article, blending colors becomes more complex as you layer progressive colors. It takes time and practice to get a seamless blend, and what do you do about making your picture's colors brighter & deeper

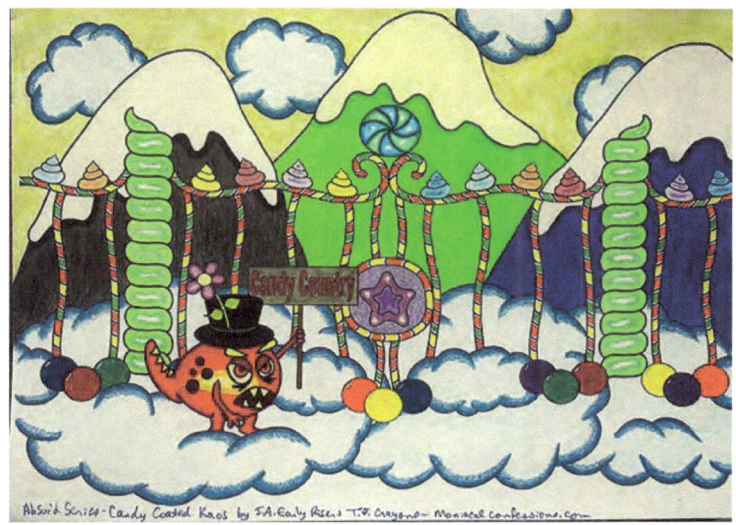

Absurd Series - Candy Coated Kaos by J.A. Early Riser T.J. Crayons - Maniacal confessions.com

other than adding several layers and using a lot of pencil?

I have tried some of the different blending techniques you see mentioned on coloring blogs & Facebook groups: using other colored pencils, a blender pencil, baby oil & Vaseline. I never got the hang of baby oil & it bled to the back of my picture, but I have had good results with the other techniques.

I recently discovered using Vaseline with my coloring. I am very impressed with the results I have been getting. While it does help with blending colors, you can also get good results from it by using it with one color. Using

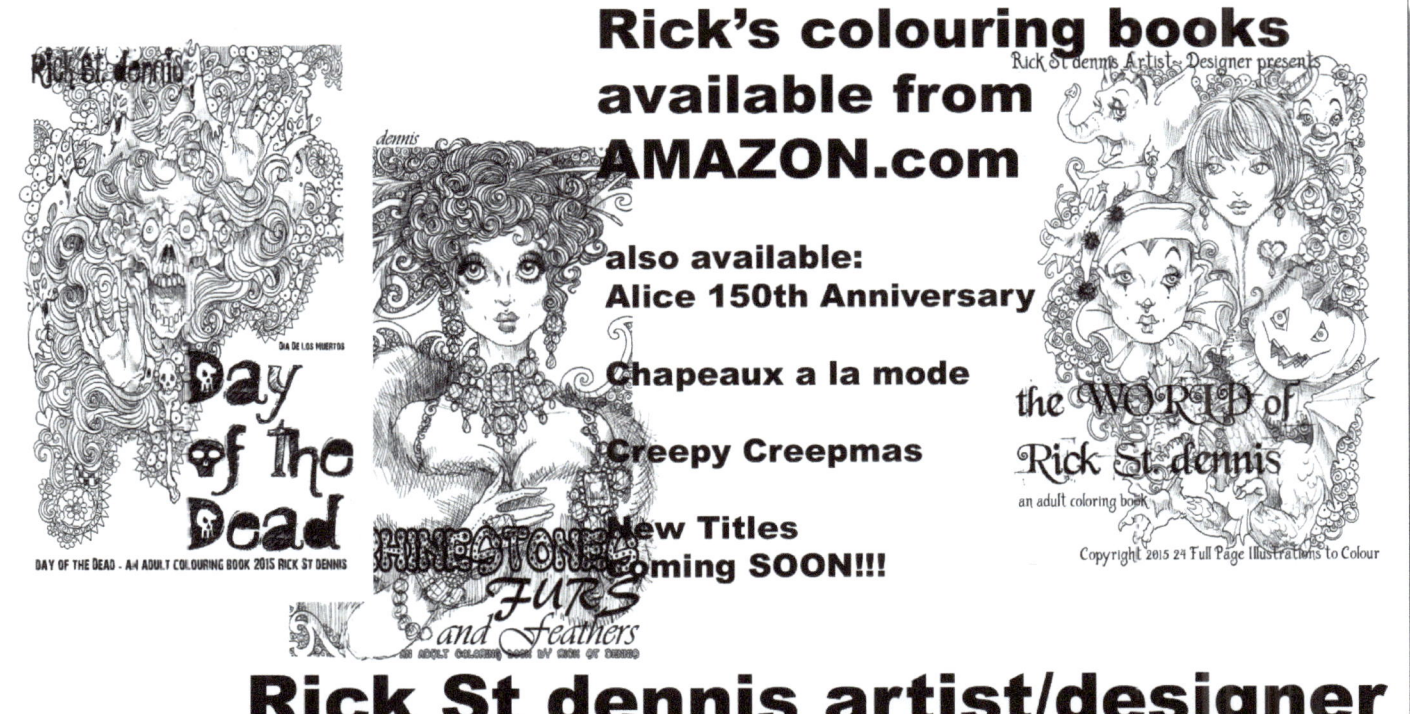

Rick's colouring books available from AMAZON.com

Rick St dennis Artist, Designer presents

also available:
Alice 150th Anniversary

Chapeaux a la mode

Creepy Creepmas

New Titles Coming SOON!!!

Day of the Dead

DAY OF THE DEAD - A4 ADULT COLOURING BOOK 2015 RICK ST DENNIS

the WORLD of Rick St. dennis
an adult coloring book
Copyright 2015 24 Full Page Illustrations to Colour

Rick St dennis artist/designer

Digital Stamps and more: http://www.zibbet.com/rick1949
Information and questions: rickstdennis@yahoo.com

Follow Rick on You Tube (how to videos) and Facebook (fan page and more)

Vaseline with your colored pencils brightens colors and fills in the natural 'valleys' in your paper so you don't have white spaces, without resorting to multiple layers & the burnishing effect this can have. Vaseline is easy to use, inexpensive, easy to find (you don't need to get it at a specialty art store) and it doesn't smell like mineral spirits do. Because you are slowly coloring over your picture with the Vaseline & blotting the excess off it can take extra time (as with any blending technique) to create your masterpiece. Any blending technique does take time and the finished result is worth the effort.

Before and after pictures using Vaseline:

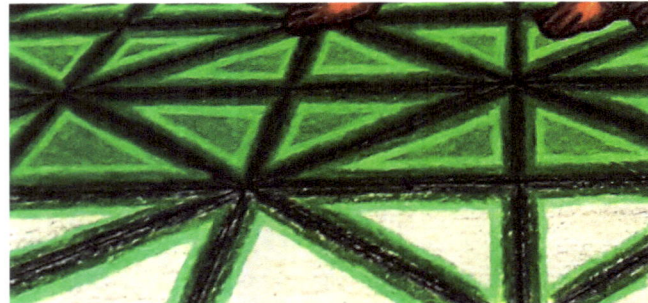

After (top squares) and before (bottom squares)

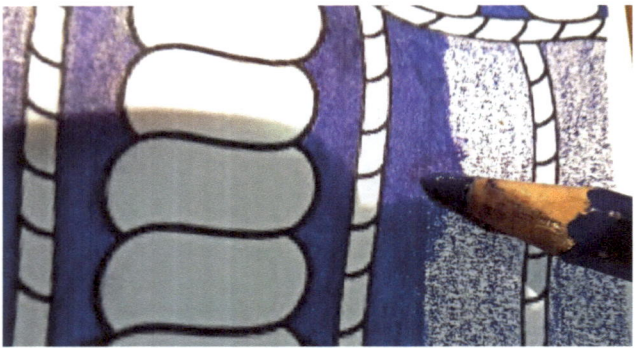

After (left) and before (right)

Materials

- A small amount of Vaseline
- Qtip (cotton buds)
- Napkin or paper towel
- Colored pencils (Note: you can also use Vaseline with a blender pencil, and possibly blender stumps –but I have not tried this. If you wish to try it, experiment on test paper before working on your good coloring projects.)
- Your picture

Technique

A quick note before we get started. You can add a little more color to your picture by coloring lightly over it after using Vaseline on it, but it will not take a deep or detailed color application after applying it. Be sure you are happy with your colors and shading before applying Vaseline.

Step 1 – Put a very small blob of Vaseline on a napkin. Depending on if you are doing blending or shadows, you can either first put a layer of colour down and then apply Vaseline, or use the Vaseline layer are the only layer.

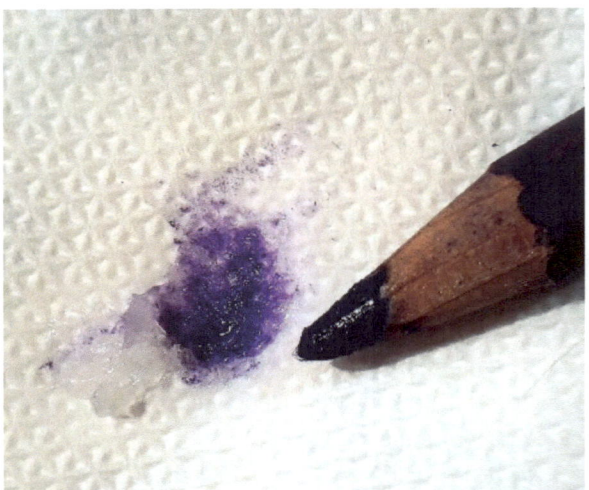

Step 2 – Roll the point of your pencil in the Vaseline lightly. You want to barely coat it, not drown it in Vaseline. Once you have a light coat, start coloring.

With practice, you will get a feel for when you start running out of Vaseline. The color won't be as saturated, and it starts to feel scratchier instead of smooth as you color. When that happens, re-coat the pencil with Vaseline.

I often find it easier to color using the side of the pencil instead of the tip, as it holds more Vaseline. That way, I have to apply it less often. I also rotate my pencil as I colour to use as much as I can before needing to reapply.

As you work, the Vaseline itself becomes colored as it picks up the pigment from the pencil. When working with different colors that you want to keep separate, you may want to clean the old colored Vaseline off your pencil by rubbing it off on the napkin, then reapply fresh Vaseline. If you are trying to blend the colors together, you can skip this step, as having the pigment in the Vaseline helps blend them.

Step 3 – As you complete small sections, use a Qtip/cotton bud to lightly rub or blot over that area to remove any extra Vaseline. Be careful not to rub into or over uncolored parts of your picture, or you will spread colored Vaseline into that area. I learned the hard way to be aware of where you have applied Vaseline (but not cleaned the excess) as you can get a bit of coloured Vaseline on your hand and transfer it to an uncoloured part of the picture on accident!

I have noticed that when I use Vaseline with a blender pencil it seems to require more applications of Vaseline than a regular colored pencil. You still get a lightening of your picture as you normally do when using a blender, but it doesn't seem to be as light as using the pencil alone.

In this example, I used Vaseline with a blender pencil. The lower left of the picture hasn't been blended yet. If you look carefully, you can see shiny streaks on the black lines. This is the excess Vaseline that I haven't yet blotted off the picture.

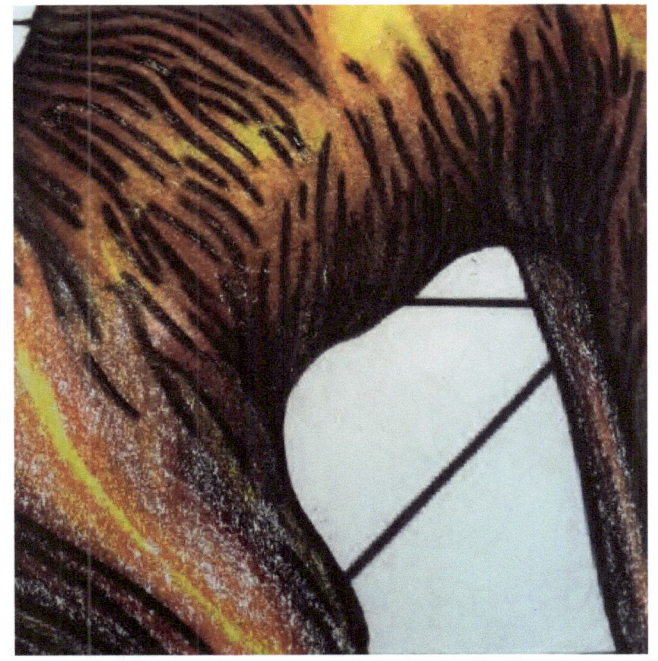

Remember - wipe any Vaseline off of your pencils with a napkin before storing them.

I have a little travel kit in a sealable plastic bag with a napkin, a few cotton buds, and a travel shampoo bottle. I put a tiny bit of Vaseline in the neck (not the main part of the bottle.) I don't want to stick my pencil all the way in and get it slippery from any Vaseline on the sides of the bottle.

If you are using only a little bit of Vaseline at a time, removing the excess and applying it by pencil (not brush or cotton bud) then you shouldn't have a problem with oily patches on the front or back of your pictures. Paper quality will vary, though, and you may see some bleed through on poor quality paper. Always practice on a scrap picture or a blank page in the back of your book before using it on a prized picture. I haven't had any tackiness on the front or any bleed through to the back of my pictures. I did the picture of the cat below using Vaseline blending for the whole picture without any problems. (Design by Jason Hamilton, from the January 2016 issue.)

This is an interesting technique that can help you get brighter colors using a material that is easy to find and relatively inexpensive. It is worth experimenting with to see how it fits in with your coloring style and how it works with your pencils.

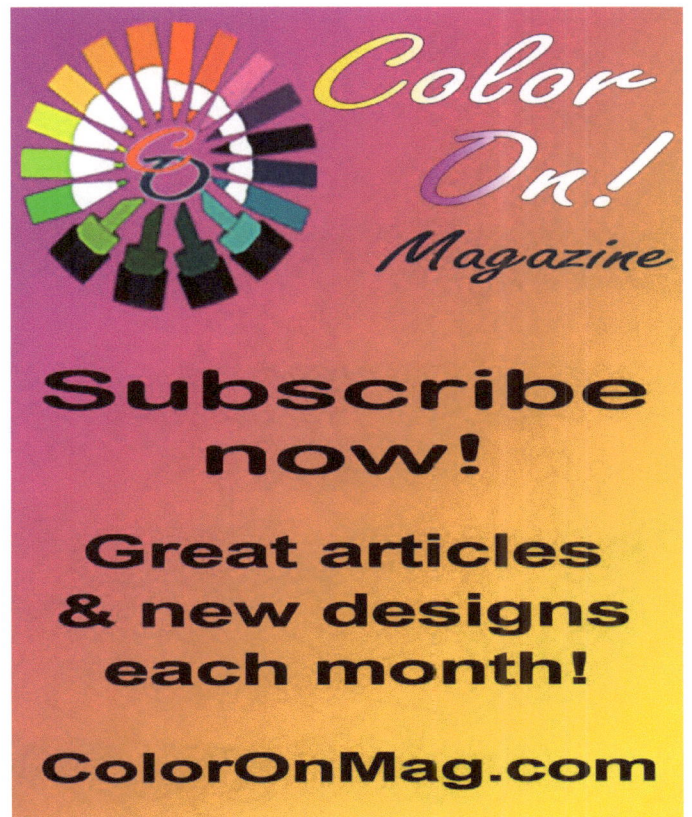

Color On! Magazine

Subscribe now!

Great articles & new designs each month!

ColorOnMag.com

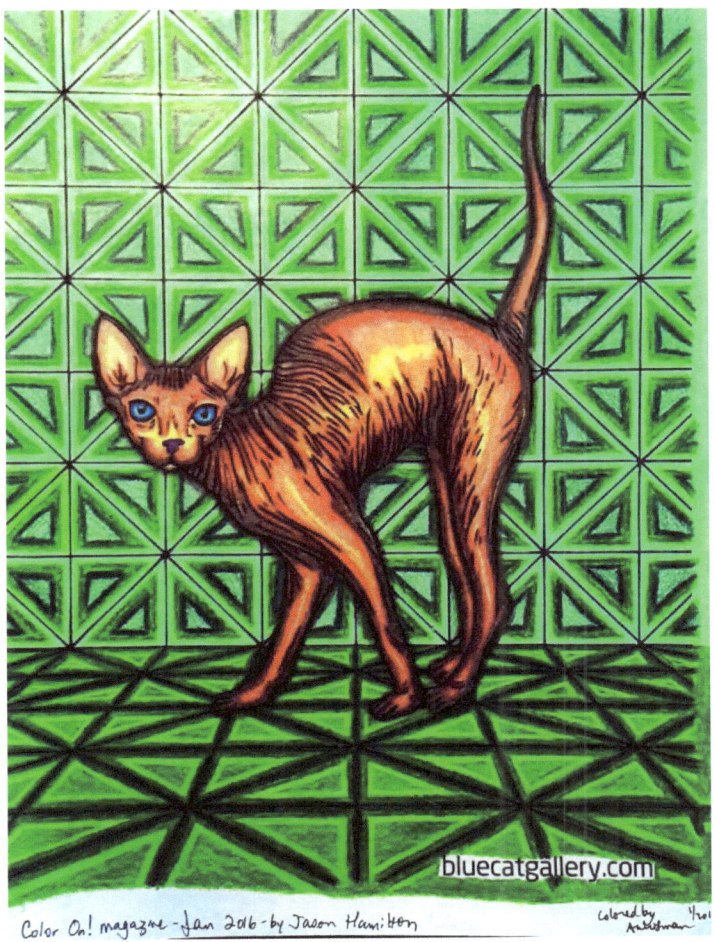

bluecatgallery.com

Color On! magazine - Jan 2016 - by Jason Hamilton   Colored by Ambletown 4/01

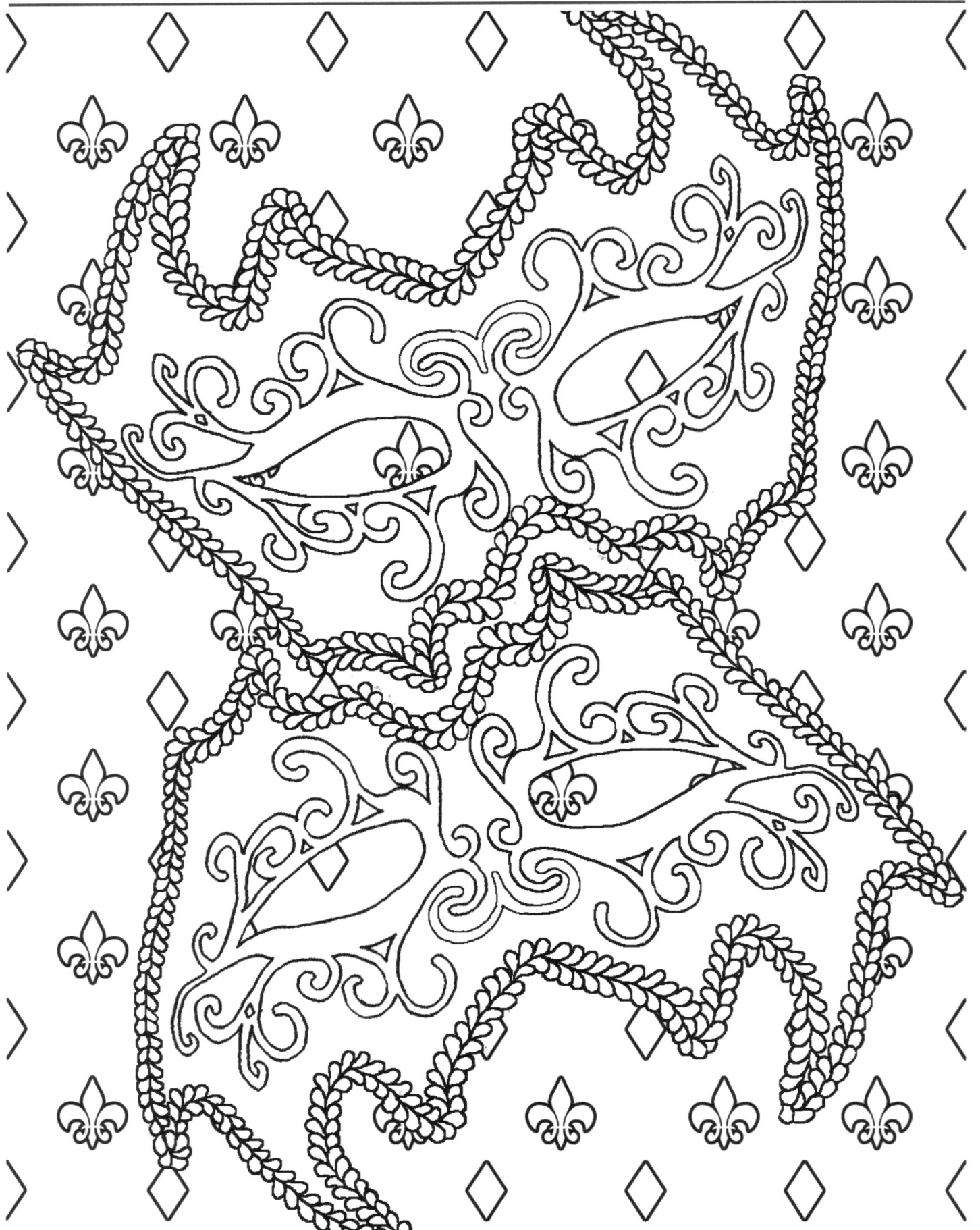

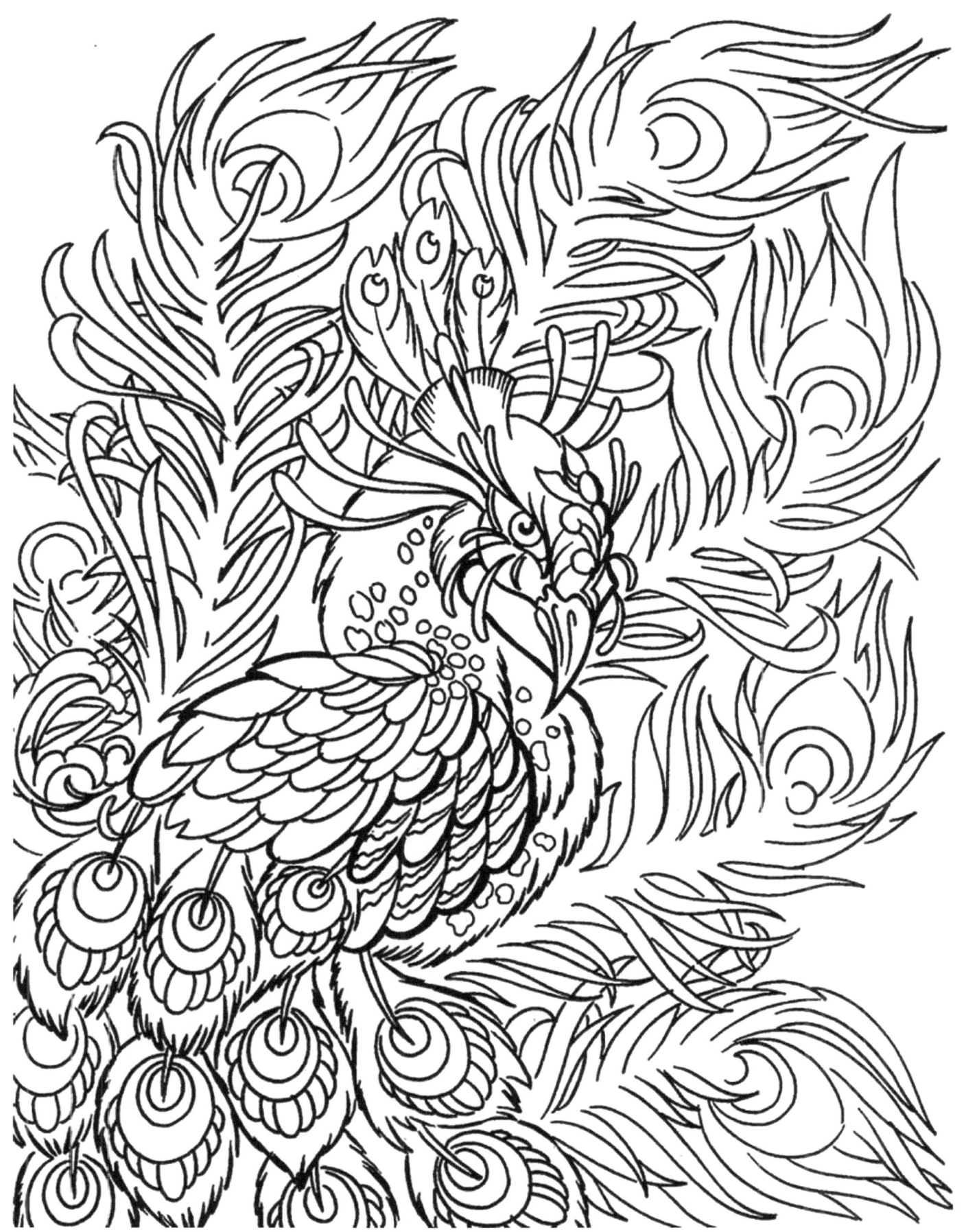

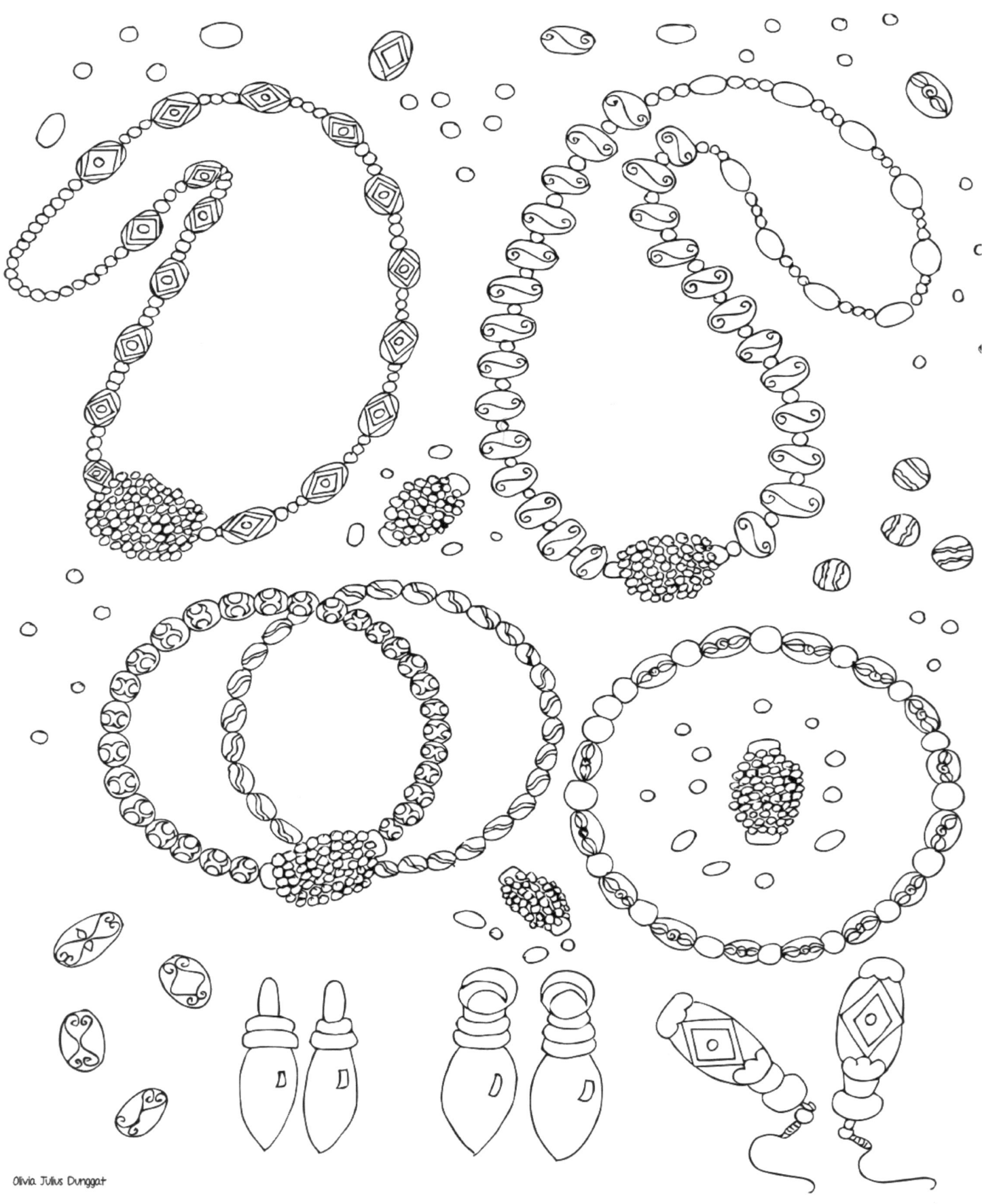

Olivia Julius Dunggat

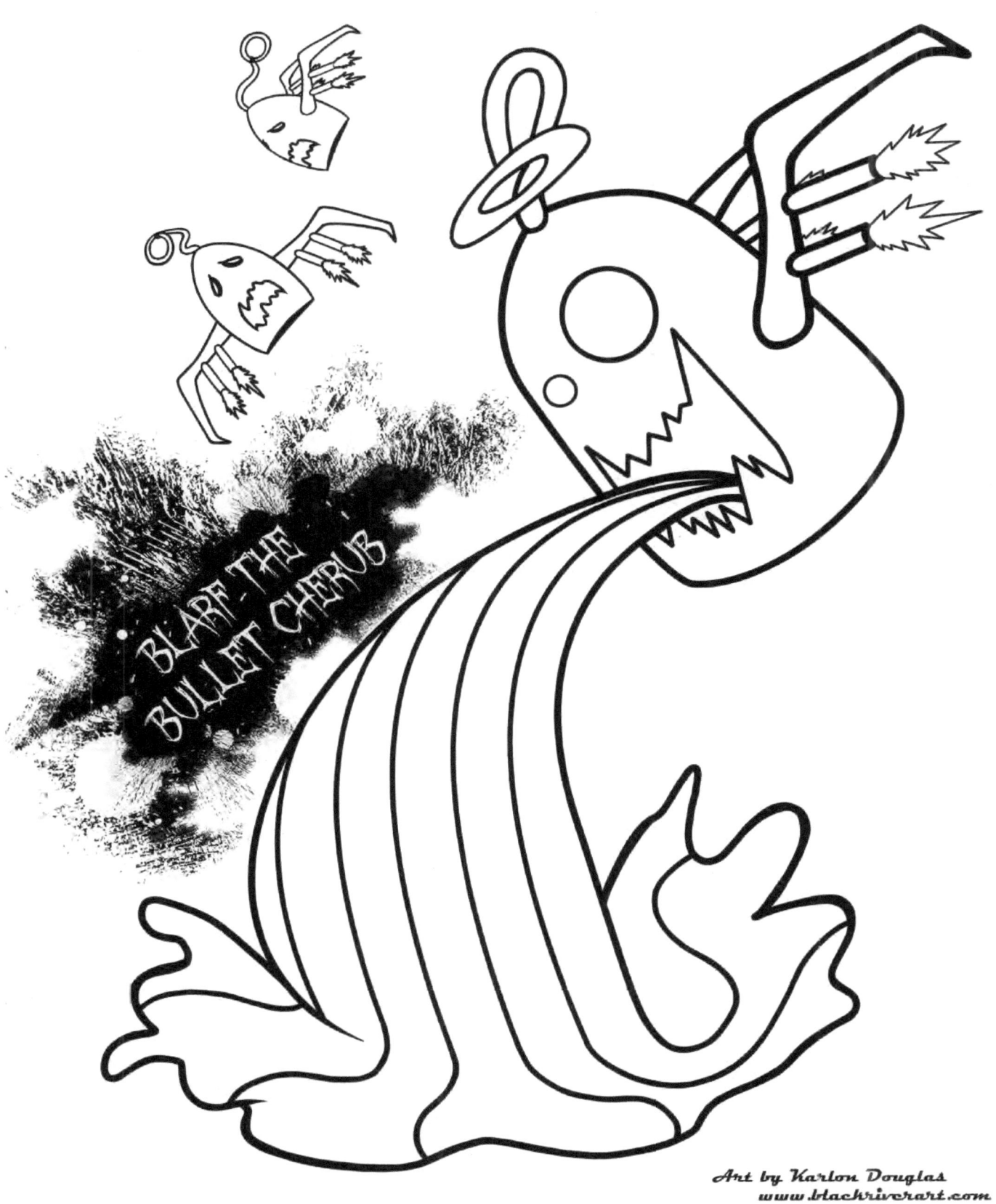

Art by Karlon Douglas
www.blackriverart.com

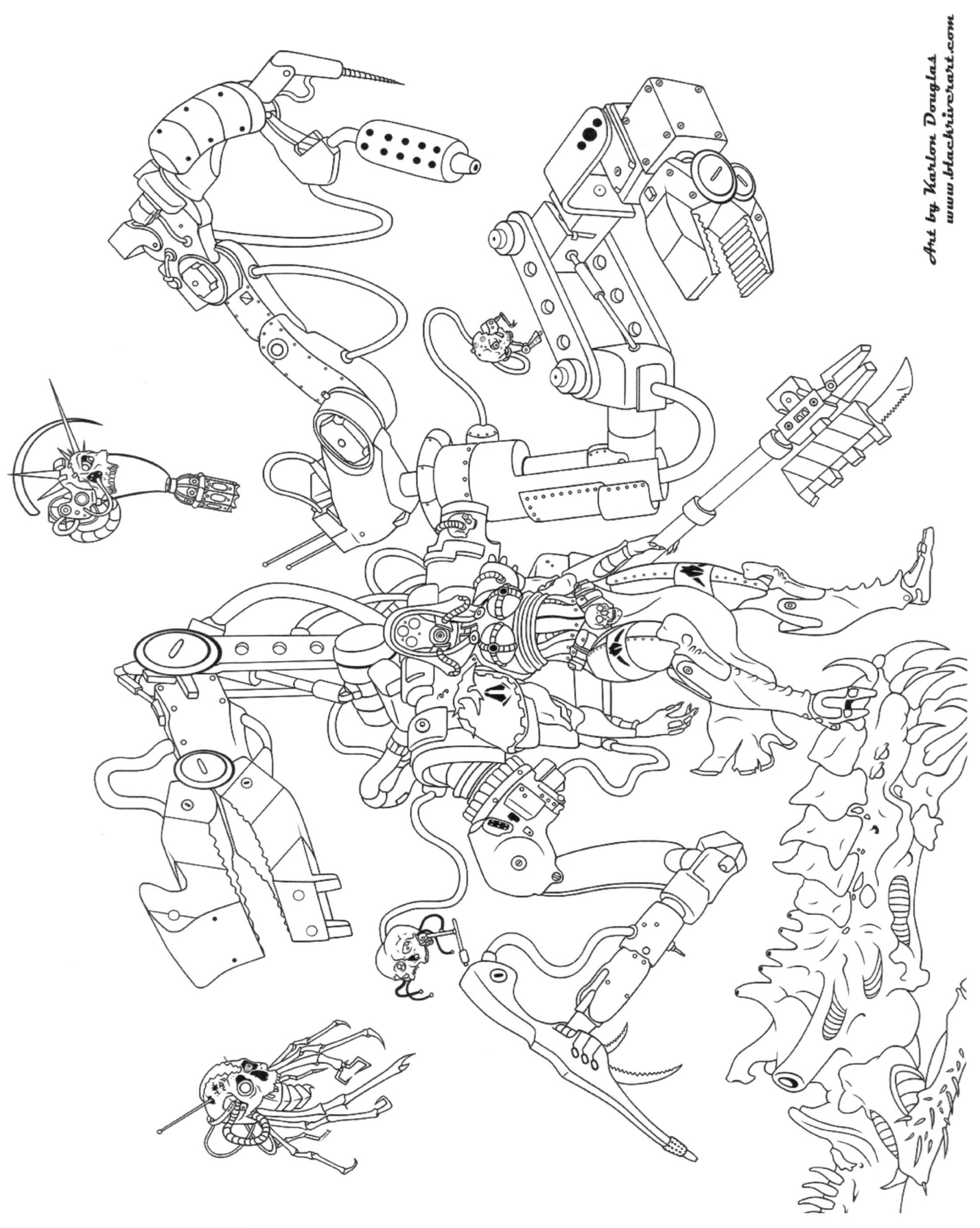

Prismacolor Premiere vs Faber Castell

...In a Nutshell

by Anisa A. Claire

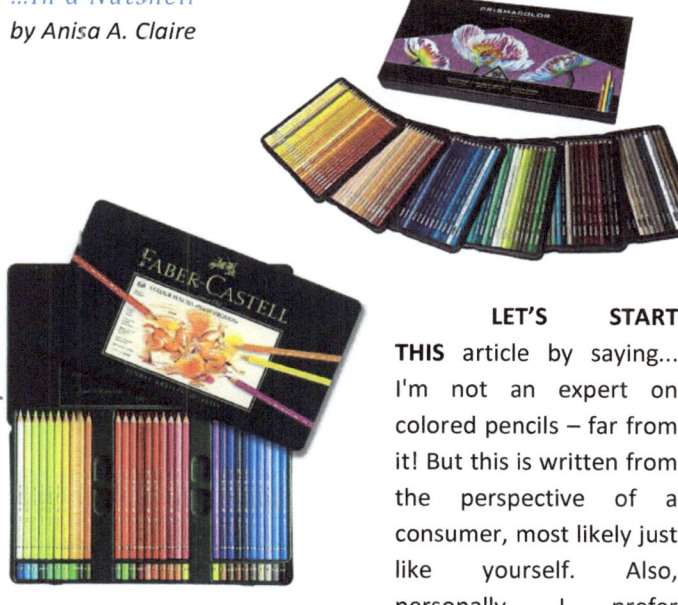

LET'S START THIS article by saying... I'm not an expert on colored pencils – far from it! But this is written from the perspective of a consumer, most likely just like yourself. Also, personally, I prefer product articles that are easy to understand and don't get too technical. Because, let's face it, if I understood the technical speak, I most likely wouldn't be reading an article on them. I'd be able to Google the specs and go 'Ah. Of course. One is a blah, blah, blah and the other is a blah, blah, blah.' So this article is written in an easier form than you may normally see in these types of reviews.

When the coloring craze hit, a whole bunch of us jumped on board. For myself, I snatched up the first book I could get my hands on, and then headed straight for the Crayola section of my local craft store. At the time, I had no idea there were even other options. Well, I'm sure I knew Crayola didn't have the market cornered, but that was my 'go-to' brand, so to speak.

After coloring a few pages, and joining a couple coloring groups on Facebook, I began hearing more and more about brands like Prismacolor and Faber-Castell. When I saw the prices, I thought... not a freaking chance! I'm happy with my Crayolas, thank you very much. But after reading more and more about them, I finally caved and purchased the Prismacolor Premiere 150-piece set. And. Loved. Every. Second. Of. It. Best purchase I'd made in 2015.

Fast forward a few months to January, and here I am now with Faber-Castell, Polychromos, the 60-piece set, as well. I am equally in love with the Faber-Castells and, so far, it has been my best purchase for 2016! However... there is a pretty big difference between them, even if the end result looks pretty similar. I have included two pictures at the end of this article, the first is completely Faber-Castell (FC), and the second is entirely Prismacolor Premiere (PP.)

So, let's start with the basics, shall we?

Packaging

PP: The 150-piece set I have comes in a cardboard-type box with a fold over, click flap. It's long and probably not as easy to pack around with you. There are three levels of trays that can be pulled out as needed.

FC: The 60-piece set I purchased comes in a tin case, it's slim and easy to pack around with you. The inside of the tin case contains two trays/levels of pencil crayons that you can pull out as needed.

Usage

PP: They are definitely a soft, wax based pencil. It's something I noticed right away going from Crayola to Prisma. They're smooth like butter – almost. Not so soft that they smear like lipstick, but soft enough that you can instantly get the full color of the pencil with minimal pressure. However, using the shade spectrum of one pencil I found to be a bit difficult in the lighter shades.

FC: These are a hard, oil based pencil. The difference is pretty incredible. You can still get the full color like you would from Prisma, but I found I had to press harder to get the same result for dark shading. That said, shading with these pencils seemed easier to control in the lighter side.

So, in shading, they seem to be reversed. Prisma is easy to get the darker shading on any individual color, but I find it trickier to get to the lighter side of the same shade. For Faber-Castell, it's extremely easy to do the lighter shading, you almost don't have to think about it, but to get the darker shades you have to apply a lot more pressure or go over an area more times than you would with Prisma.

Blending

PP: With Prisma, I find I have to use a blending pencil no matter how light or dark my shading is, it always needs to be smoothed out. Sometimes I get a bit of a wax build up with the Prismas.

FC: If you use a blending pencil, you'll find they agree with this brand. They blend with ease. That said, I would *almost* say you don't even need a blending pencil with Faber-Castell if you're doing lighter shading. They're really that good. If you're going into darker, or bolder shading, then a blending pencil does help to smooth out the transition. Because they're oil based, not wax based, there is no wax build-up. That's nice.

Sharpening

PP: I am constantly sharpening my Prisma pencils. They do break here and there. I probably burn through these way faster than I do any other pencil crayon I own.

FC: I rarely sharpen my Faber-Castell pencils. They stay sharp and I don't burn them up quickly in comparison to Prisma.

Pricing

PP: It's really starting to vary because of all the sales Amazon.com or Amazon.ca has lately. I bought my 150-piece pack for $150. One week later, the same pack dropped to $99. You can replace them individually, typically, in a place like Michaels or Deserres for a pretty penny.

FC: I got my Faber Castell's on sale at Deserres for $129, which at the time was around $50 cheaper than what Amazon was offering. So definitely watch out for sales and check a few different places before purchasing either brand.

Remember, this is written from 'just another consumer's' point of view. I'll end by saying that I honestly love both brands, but for different reasons. I love to color bright, bold pictures, mainly, but sometimes dip into the more 'serious' shading. For my extremely bright pictures, I would use Prisma's, but for my more serious pictures... I would definitely use Faber-Castell.

Prisma's are cheaper in initial price, however, because of the amount you have to sharpen them, mixed in with the breakage that occurs sometimes, I would say that Faber-Castell requires less sharpening, causing the two brands to almost be the same price value.

Wax build up aside, I still love Prisma. It's true. I do. I wouldn't give them up for anything. That said, I also love my Faber-Castell's, though I probably use them significantly less than my Prisma's.

Well, I hope this helps you at least a little bit. I know it's not a super technical article, but it does break down the basics. My final recommendation would depend on what type of colorist you are. If you enjoy heavy coloring with bright, bold colors, definitely go with Prisma. If you're more into natural shading and realistic-looking pictures, I would highly recommend Faber Castell.

Until next time, folks!

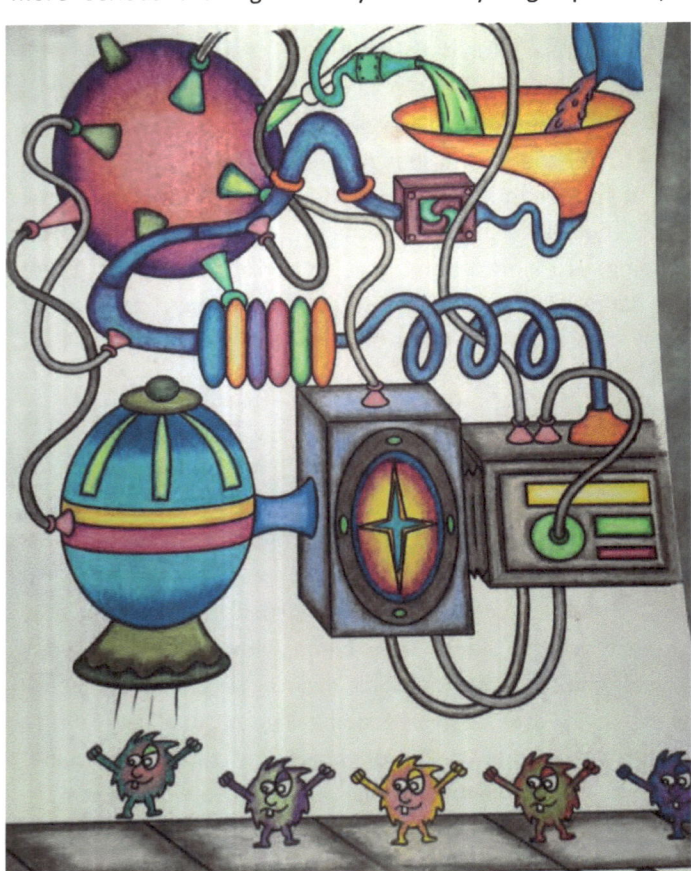

COLORED WITH FABER CASTELL
Picture from Absur'd Candy Coated Kaos

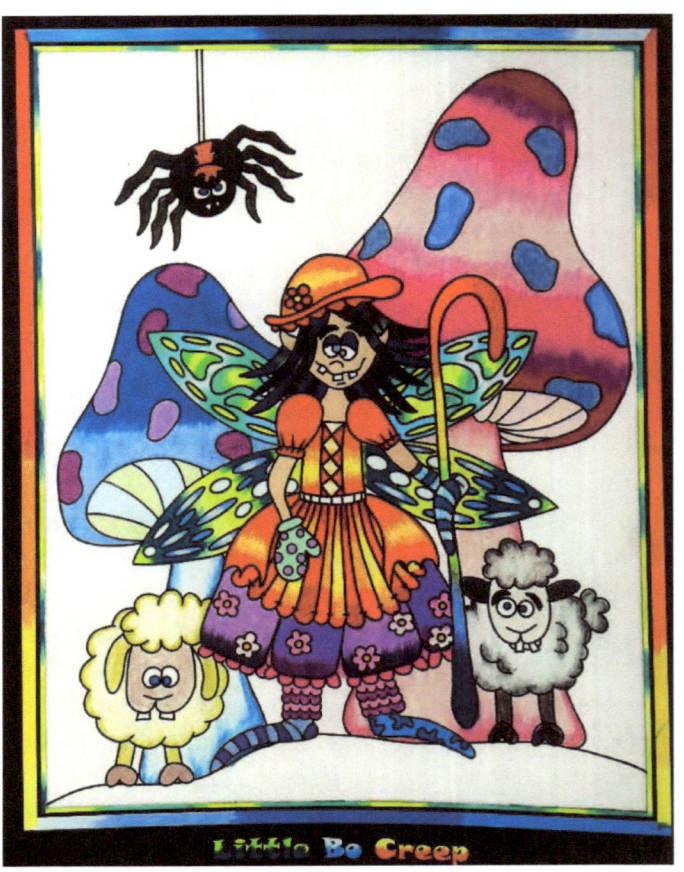

COLORED WITH PRISMA PREMIERE
Picture from Absur'd Feral Fairy Tales

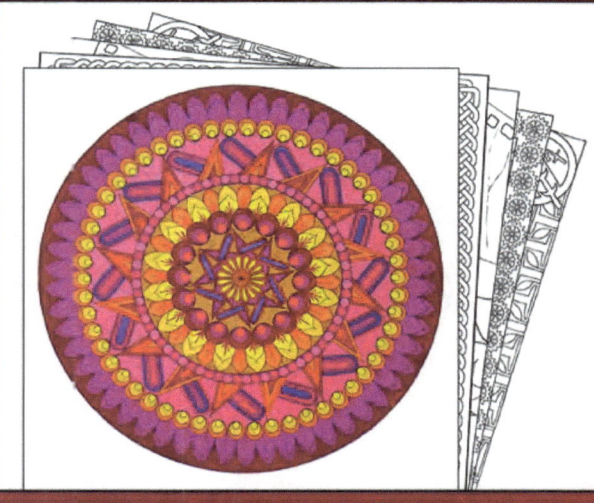

Dragons, Knots, Bots and More!

(Coloring Passions Volume 1)

by Mary J. Winters-Meyer

Over 25 fun, geeky designs!

Frolicking dragons, Celtic knots, mandalas, steampunk, nanobots, and more!

Buy your copy now on Amazon!

http://amzn.to/1WXYqLe

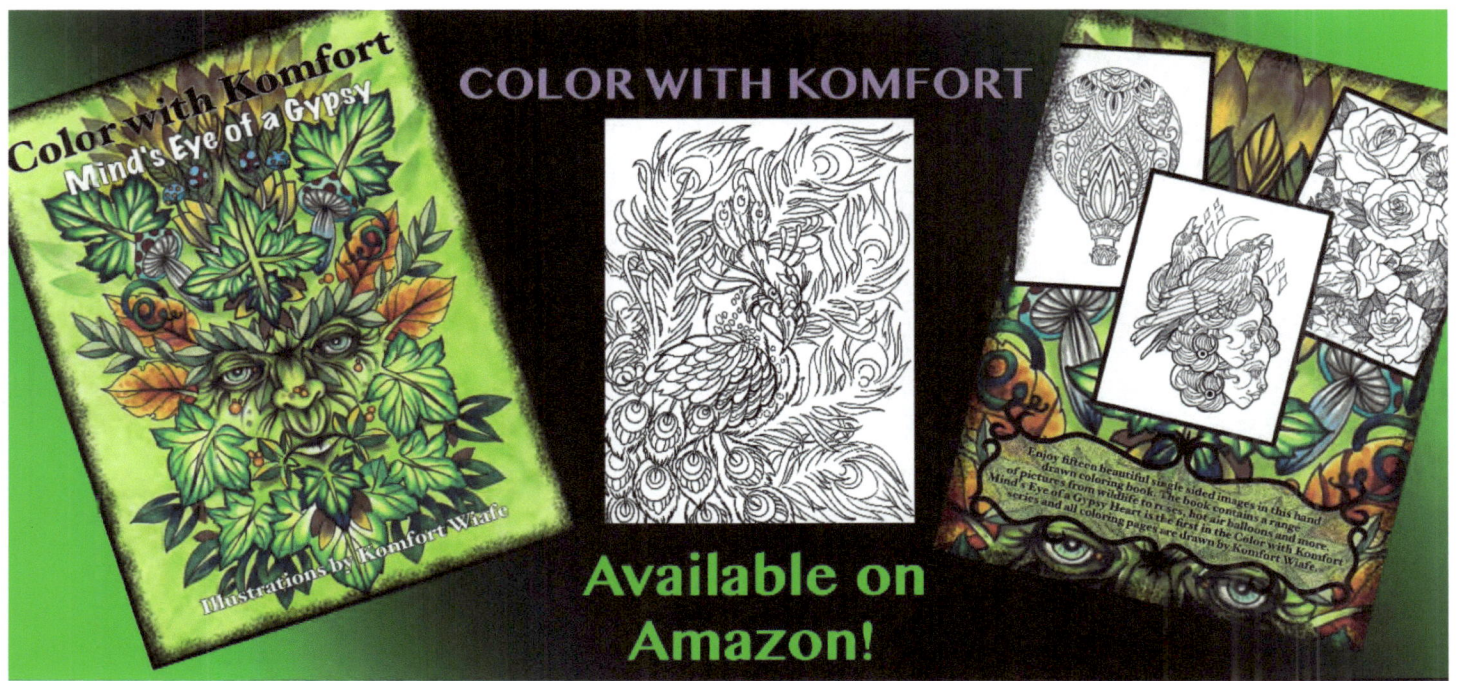

Color with Komfort
Mind's Eye of a Gypsy

Illustrations by Komfort Wiafe

COLOR WITH KOMFORT

Enjoy fifteen beautiful single sided images in this hand drawn coloring book. The book contains a range of pictures from wildlife to roses, hot air balloons and more. Mind's Eye of a Gypsy Heart is the first in the Color with Komfort series and all coloring pages are drawn by Komfort Wiafe.

Available on Amazon!

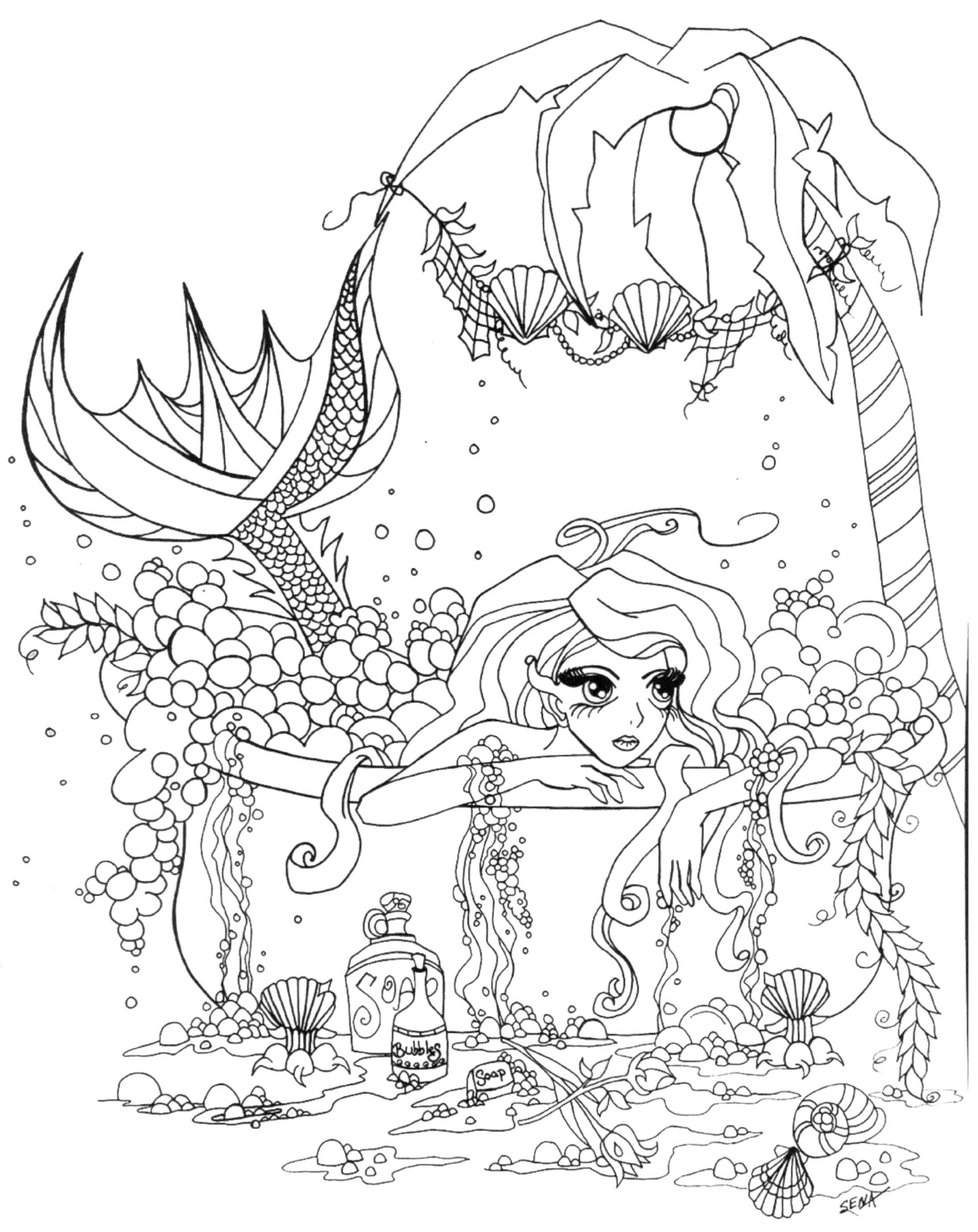

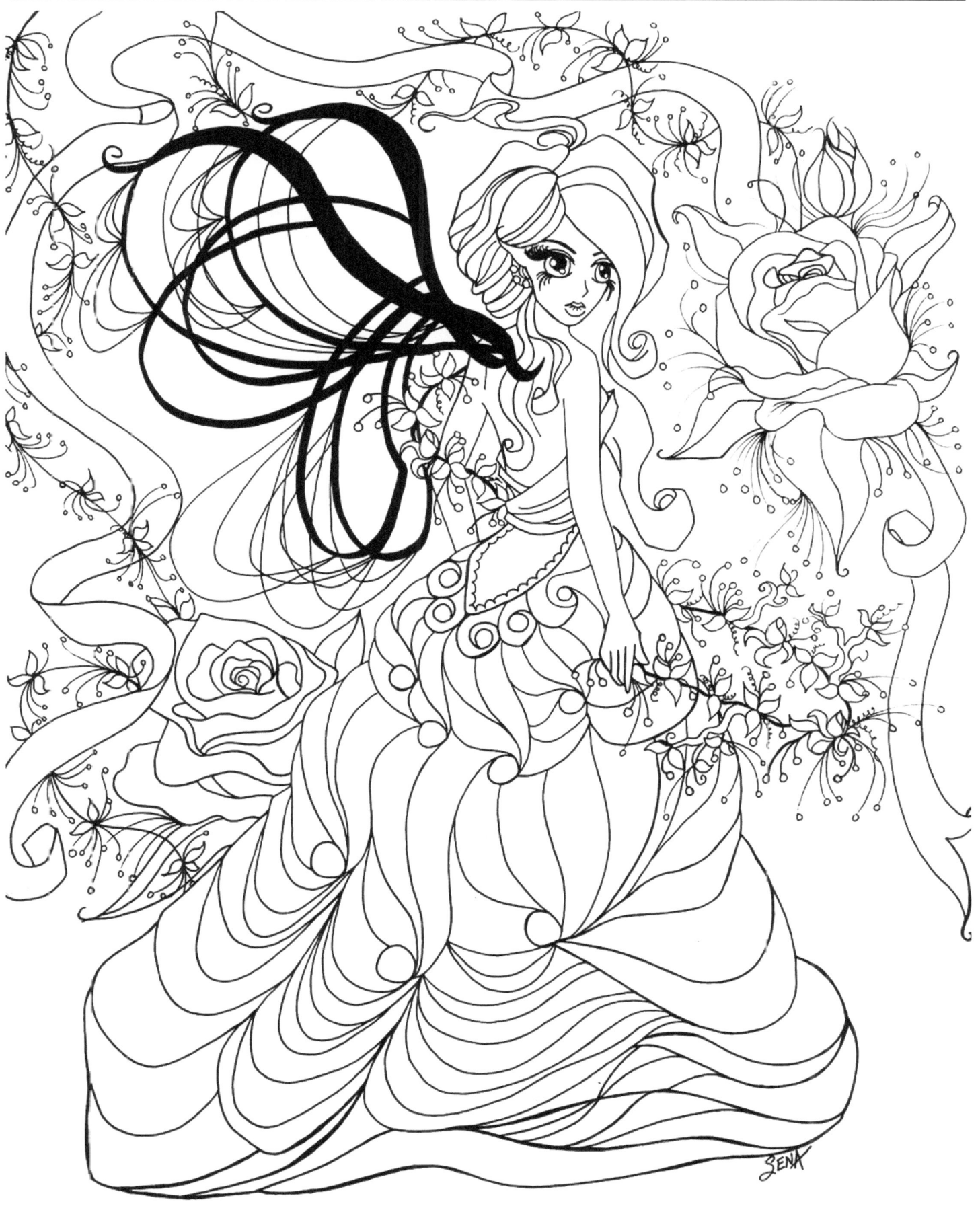

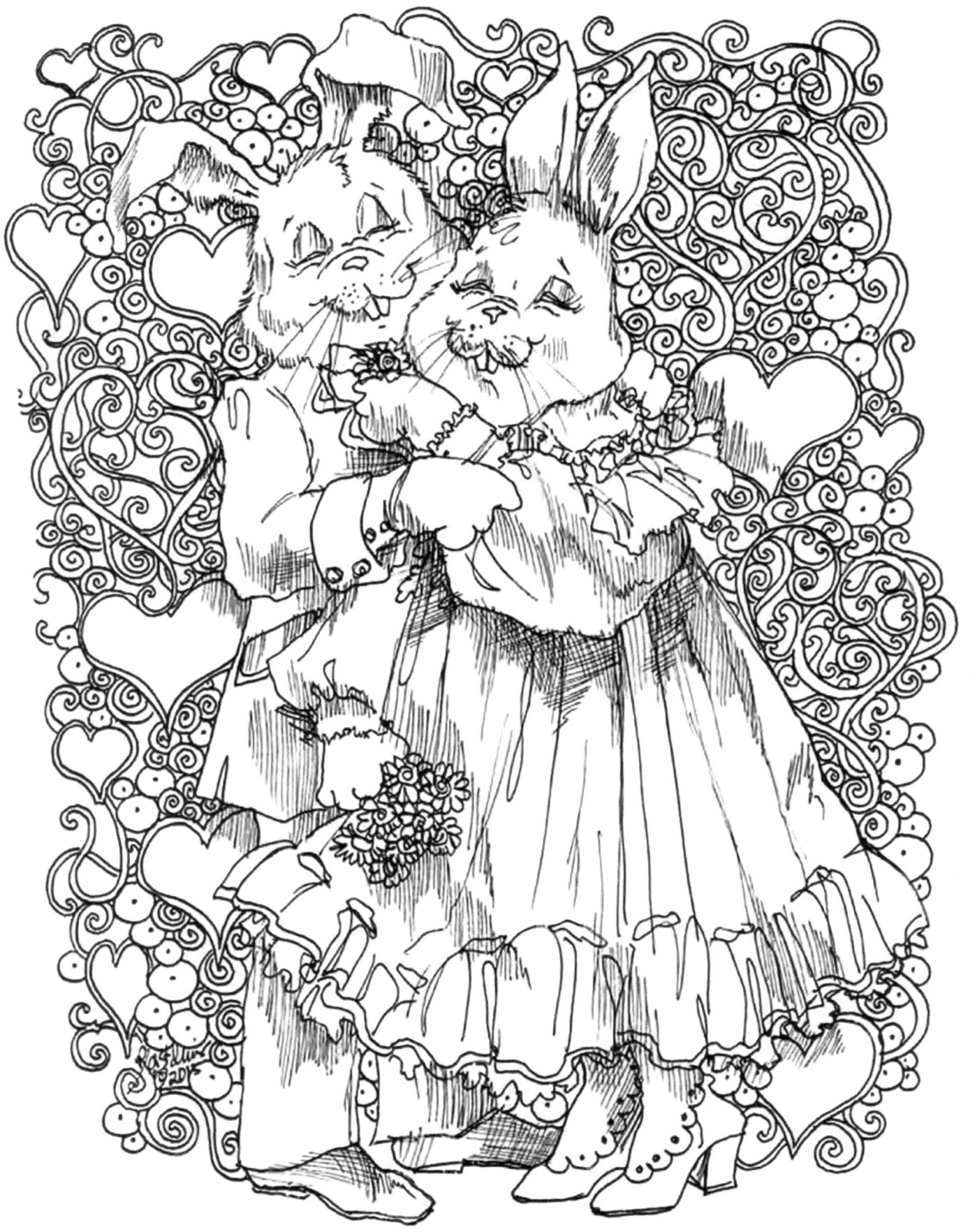

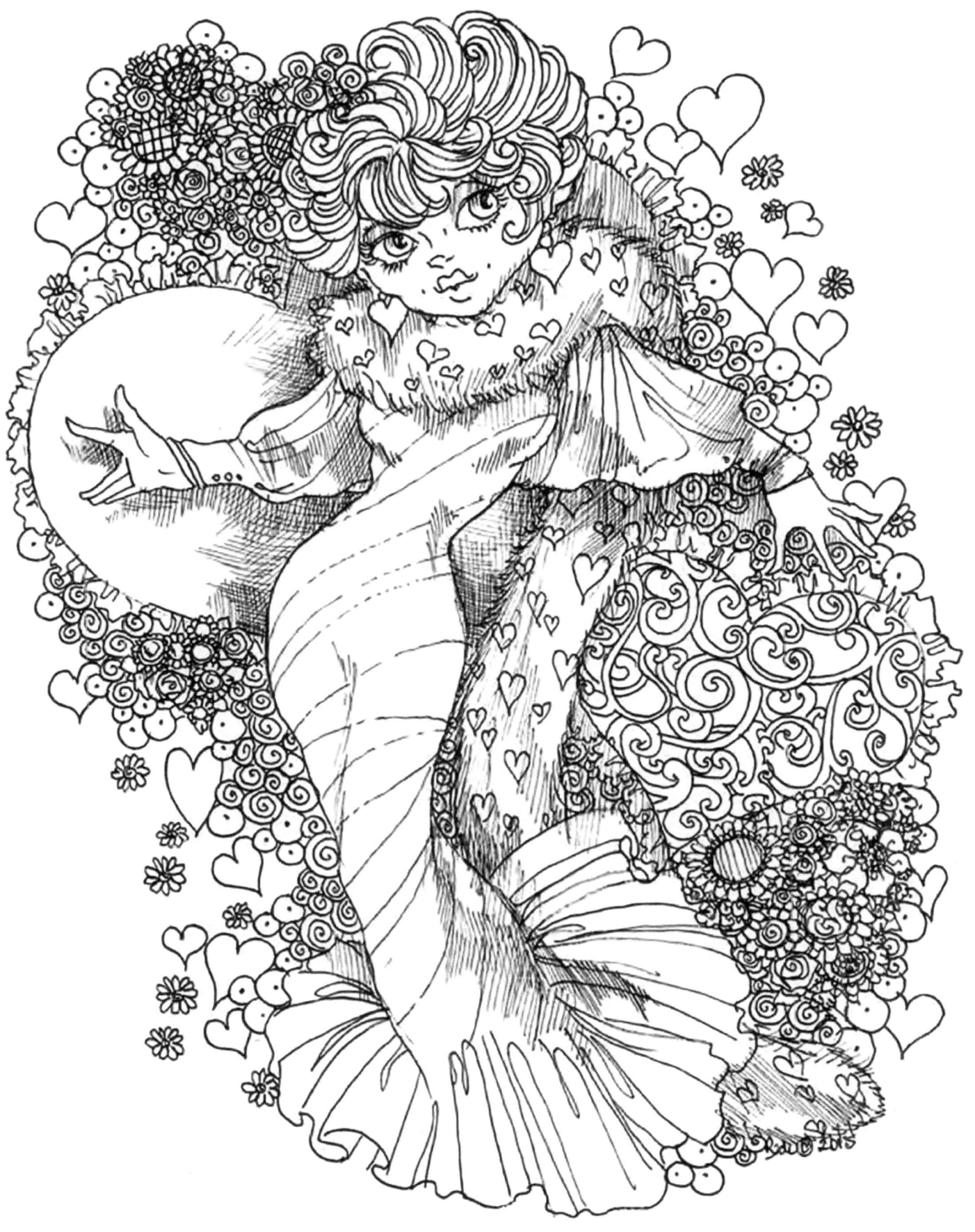

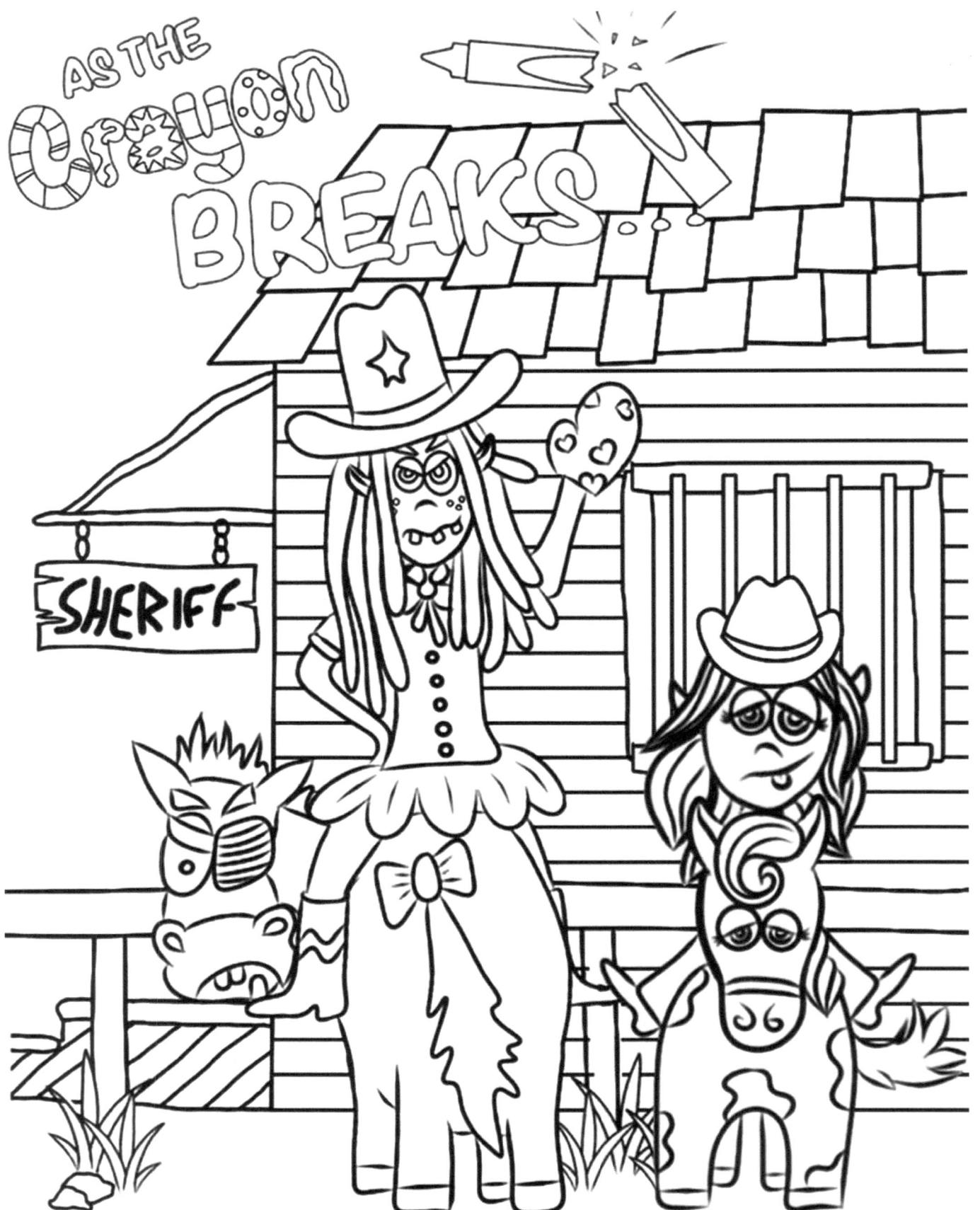

Introducing... Marshal Early Riser and the Gallumphing Grammar Gal!
Saving the West one crayon-crazed villain at a time.

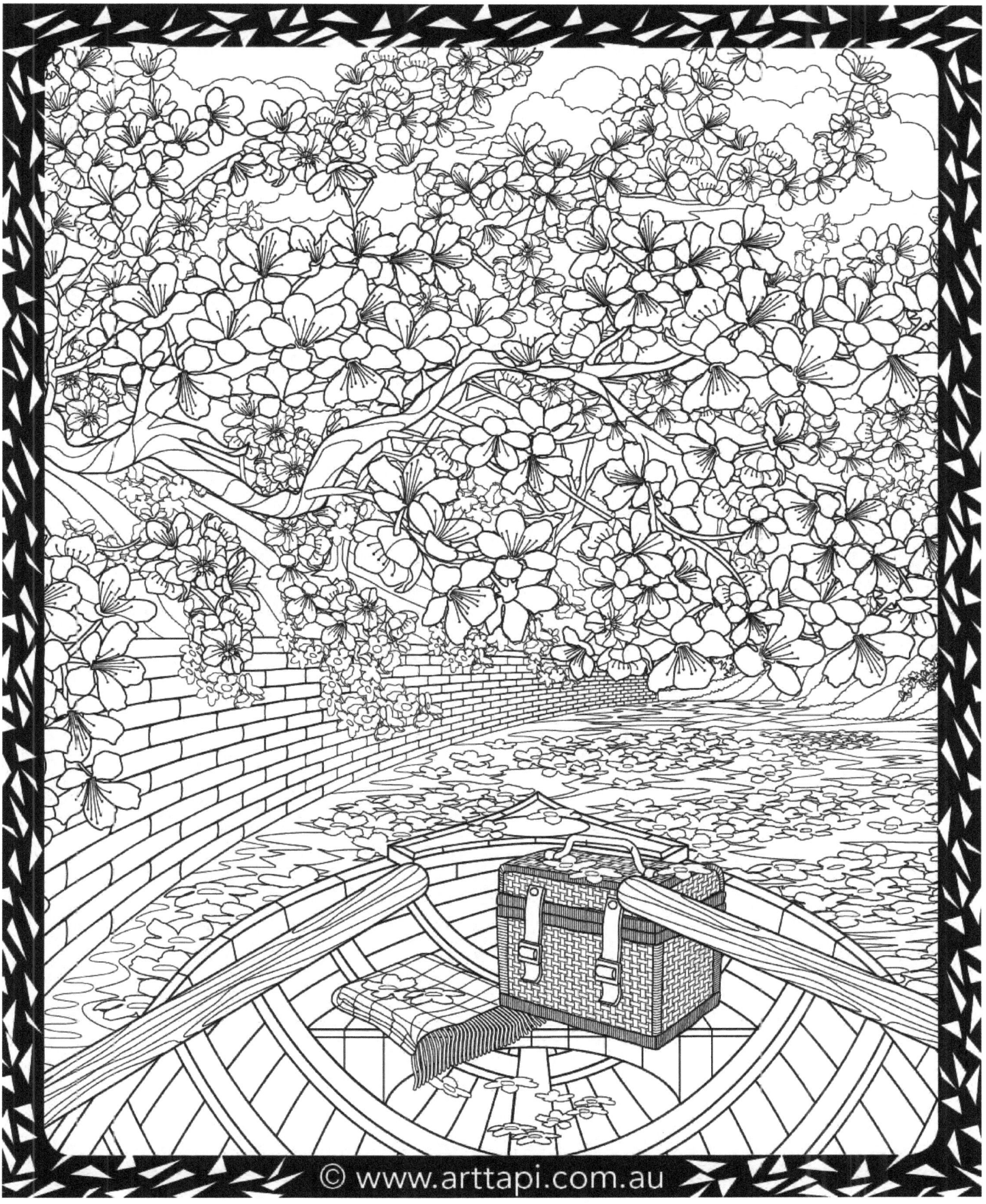

© www.arttapi.com.au

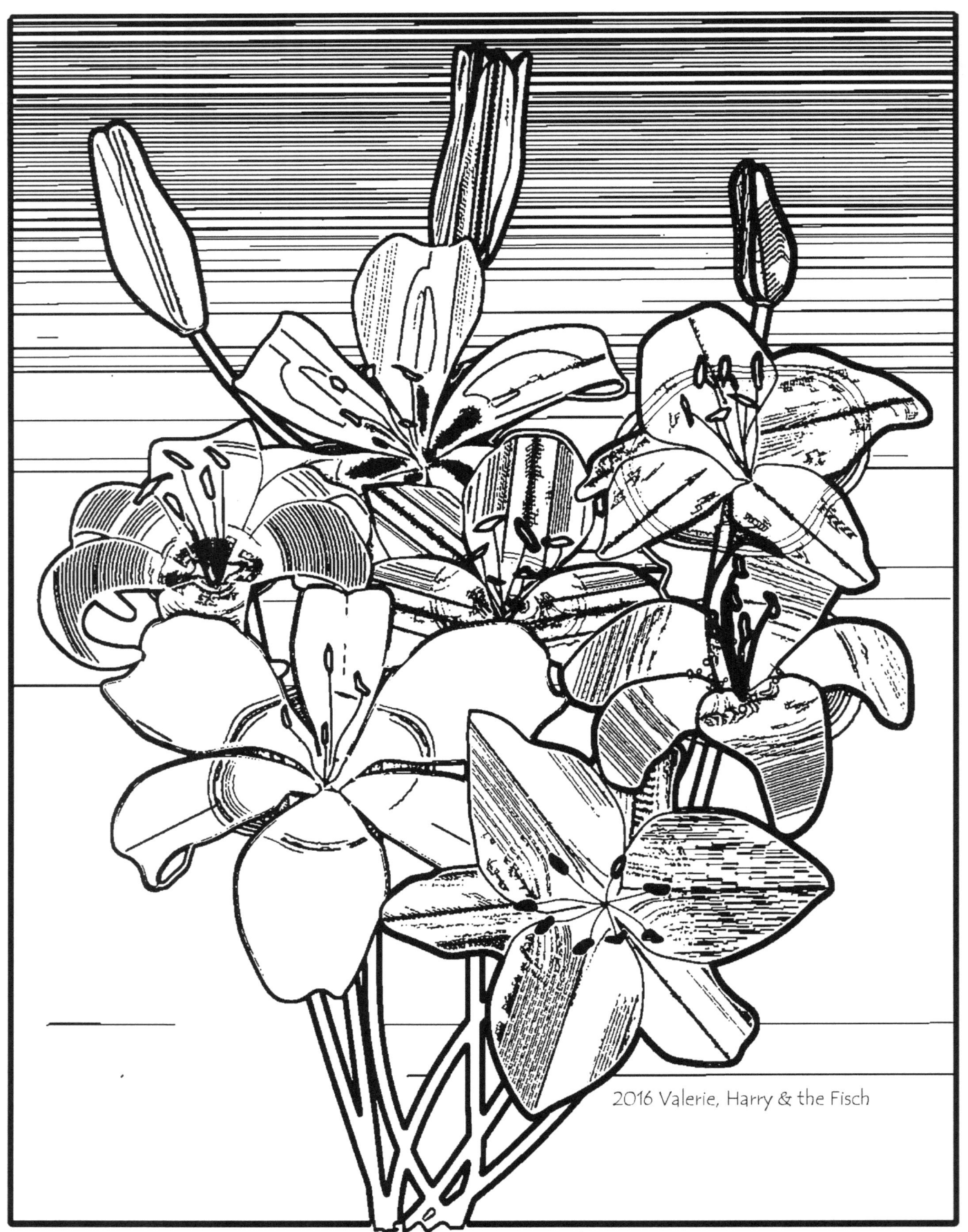

2016 Valerie, Harry & the Fisch

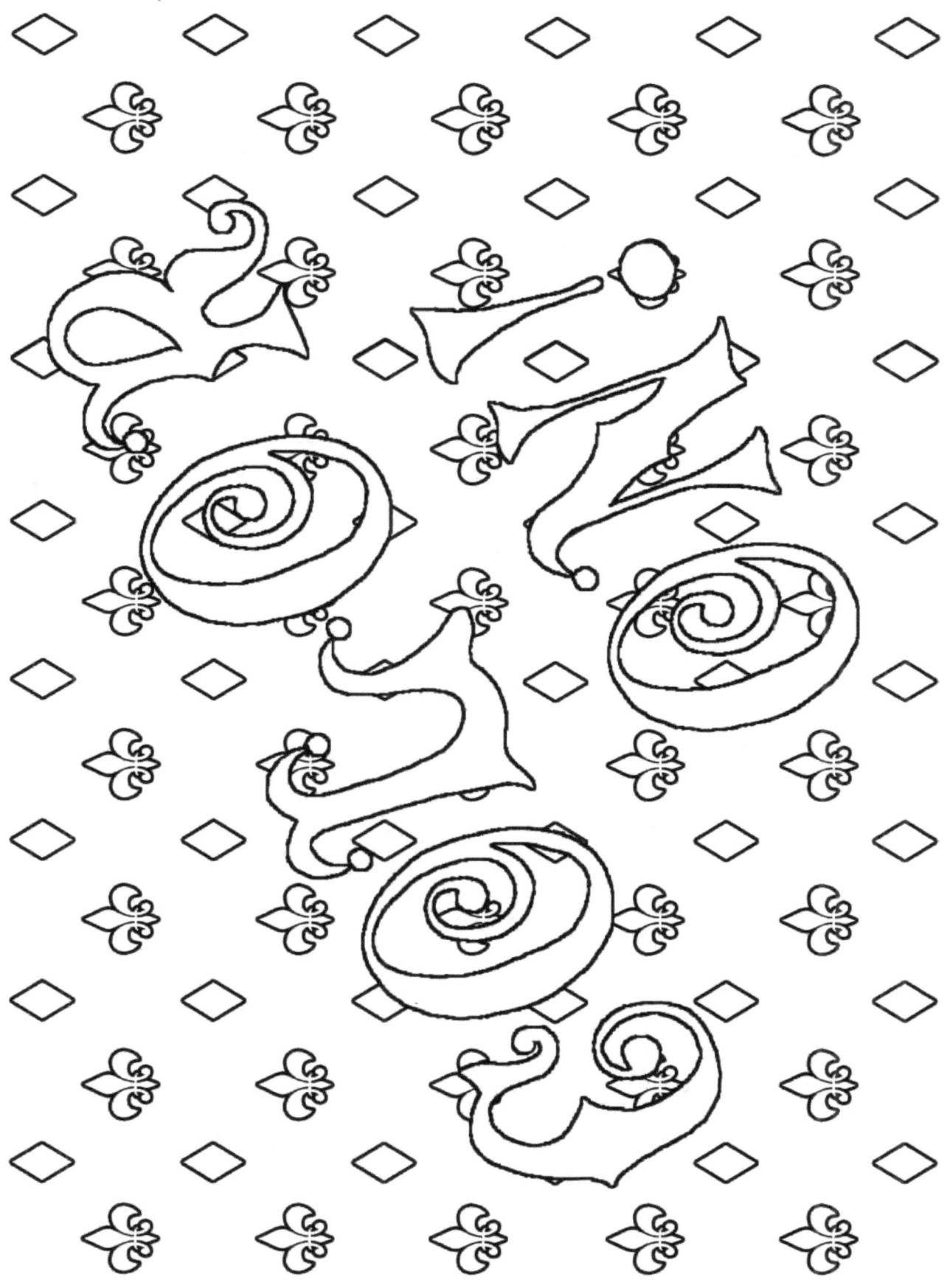

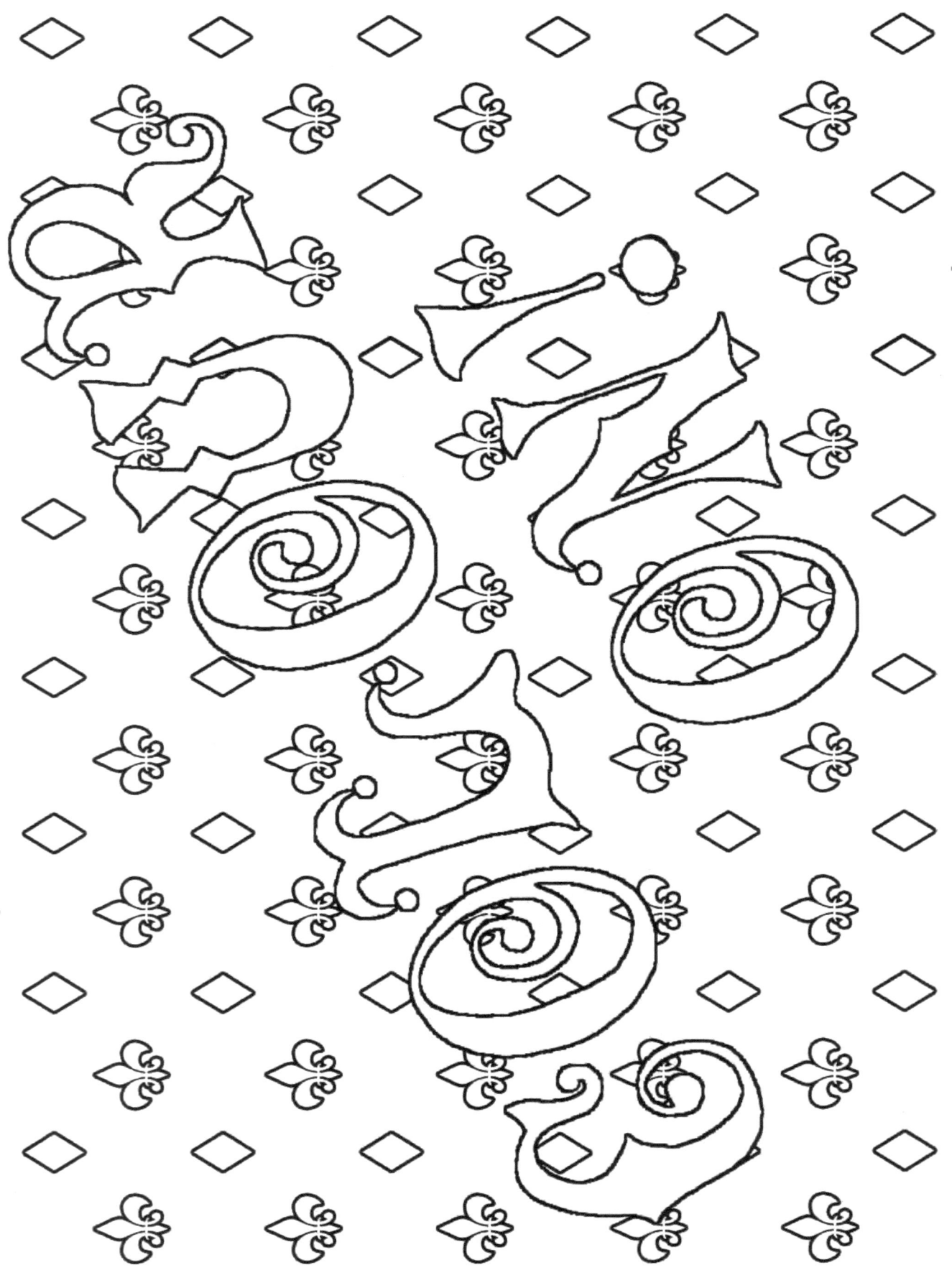

www.ingramcontent.com/pod-product-compliance
Lightning Source LLC
Chambersburg PA
CBHW040754200526
45159CB00025B/2095